Filmguide to

The Grapes of Wrath

D0901865

INDIANA UNIVERSITY PRESS FILMGUIDE SERIES
Harry Geduld and Ronald Gottesman,
General Editors

Filmguide to

The
Grapes of Wrath

WARREN FRENCH

INDIANA UNIVERSITY PRESS
Bloomington London

Copyright © 1973 by Indiana University Press
All rights reserved
No part of this book may be reproduced or utilized in any form
or by any means, electronic or mechanical, including photocopying
and recording, or by any information storage and retrieval system,
without permission in writing from the publisher. The Association
of American University Presses Resolution on Permissions constitutes
the only exception to this prohibition.

Published in Canada by Fitzhenry & Whiteside Limited, Don Mills, Ontario
Library of Congress catalog card number: 72–88912
ISBN: 0–253–39303–5 cl.   0–253–39304–3 pa.
Manufactured in the United States of America

for Don and Ken and the
great days of "Showtime" on KCUR–FM

contents

preface

This book—like all I have written—is based upon the premise that criticism should stimulate, not suppress discussion. I have tried to advance some provocative theories, raise more issues than I attempt to resolve, in the hope of getting others thinking and talking about *The Grapes of Wrath*. Much film criticism has been dogmatic and pontifical. It is time that this important art form was dignified with a criticism that explores films instead of using them as springboards for personal vendettas.

Rather than clutter the text with footnotes, I have incorporated essential references into the text and keyed them to the bibliography.

This book might never have gotten off the ground without the encouragement and assistance of Donald Pease, though he cannot be held responsible for the perversity of any views expressed.

WARREN FRENCH

credits

THE GRAPES OF WRATH
Twentieth Century-Fox, 1940

Director	John Ford
Producer	Darryl F. Zanuck
Associate Producer-Scenarist	Nunnally Johnson, from John Steinbeck's novel, *The Grapes of Wrath* (1939)
Assistant Director	Edward O'Fearna
Director of Photography	Gregg Toland
Art Directors	Richard Day, Mark Lee Kirk
Set Decorator	Thomas Little
Musical Score	Alfred Newman

(Song "Red River Valley" played on accordion by Dan Borzage)

Editor	Robert Simpson
Sound Directors	George Leverett, Roger Heman
Sound Effects Director	Robert Parrish
Time: 128 minutes	Opened at the Rivoli Theatre, New York, January 24, 1940.

CAST

The Joad Party

Tom	Henry Fonda	*Noah*	Frank Sully
Ma	Jane Darwell	*Al*	O. Z. Whitehead
Pa	Russell Simpson	*Rosasharn*	Dorris Bowdon
Grampa	Charley Grapewin	*Connie Rivers*	Eddie Quillan
Granma	Zeffie Tilbury	*Ruthie*	Shirley Mills
Uncle John	Frank Darien	*Winfield*	Darryl Hickman

Others

Casy	John Carradine	*Policeman*	Ward Bond
Muley Graves	John Qualen	*Floyd*	Paul Guilfoyle
Caretaker at Wheat Patch	Grant Mitchell	*Wilkie*	Charles D. Brown

2 ·

outline:

The Grapes of Wrath

Films are organized in shots, scenes, sequences. Ronald Gottesman and Harry M. Geduld in *Guidebook to Film* (1972) define a *shot* as "a piece of film that has been exposed, without cuts or interruptions, in a single running of the camera" (pp. 225–26). The camera may move in any direction during a shot, but "within any single shot there is no discontinuity of time or space." A *scene* is a group of shots in which the action is continuous (though flashbacks or flash forwards may be inserted)–the basic narrative unit of the film. A sequence is defined as "an arrangement of shots or scenes which together provide a coherent unit in the development of a film story or theme" (p. 225).

Shot-by-shot analysis of a motion picture is possible, as Theodore Huff's remarkable listing of the 1,716 separate shots in D. W. Griffith's *Intolerance* indicates, but it is difficult to use and confusing if only a few feet are lost from a print.

This outline of *The Grapes of Wrath* divides the film into fifty identifiable scenes that may be grouped into fifteen sequences lasting from one minute to twenty-five minutes. The heart of the picture is the three contrasting sequences at camps in California, which account for 61 of the film's 128 minutes.

Sequence One—Tom Joad's Return (10 minutes). Scene 1. A long-shot of a man (Tom Joad) coming over the horizon and walking down an Oklahoma country highway. 2. Outside a roadside restaurant he asks a truck driver for a lift. 3. In the cab of the truck, he tells the driver that he has just been paroled from the penitentiary, where he was serving a term for homicide. 4. Alighting from the truck, Tom finds Casy, the preacher who baptized him, singing under a willow tree. Casy explains he is no longer a preacher, and Tom tells about his four years in prison. 5. Casy describes Tom's father's behavior at a baptizing as Tom and Casy walk toward the old Joad cabin. A dust storm comes up.

Sequence Two—The Deserted Joad Cabin (12 minutes). Scene 6. Tom and Casy find the cabin deserted. Muley Graves, a neighbor, appears and tells about the sharecroppers being "tractored off" by the big owners. Two flashbacks reveal how Muley was dispossessed. He tells Tom that the Joad family is at Uncle John's preparing to move to California. 7. Tom, Casy, and Muley are later obliged to hide out from armed watchmen who are hunting for Muley.

Sequence Three—Off to California (14 minutes). Scene 8. Tom is reunited with the family and learns their plans for the trip. The reunion is interrupted by two men in a car who warn Uncle John that the tractors are coming through his farm the next day. 9. The Joads load the truck for the trip, while Ma reminisces over her few souvenirs. 10. When Grampa refuses to go on the trip, he has to be put to sleep with soothing syrup. Casy is invited to join the party, and the truck departs. 11. Outraged, Ma Joad refuses to look back at the farm.

Sequence Four—Grampa's Death (5 minutes). Scene 12. A montage showing the Joad truck crossing Oklahoma, among many others, while Grampa suffers inside. 13. Grampa is unloaded from the truck and dies. 14. Tom reads a note that will be buried with Grampa, explaining that he wasn't killed; Casy says "a few words" over the grave.

Sequence Five—At a Campground: Bad News (4 minutes). Scene 15. The campers along the way are being entertained by Rosasharn's husband Connie, who is singing a folk song. A man returning from California laughs scornfully at the Joads' optimism and explains that he saw his wife and two sons starve in California. The group breaks up much distressed.

Sequence Six—At a Truck Stop: Good People (5 minutes). Scene 16. Following another montage of highway scenes, the Joads are treated contemptuously by a gas station attendant. 17. Inside a hamburger joint, where a waitress is joshing two truck drivers, Pa Joad attempts to buy a loaf of bread. When the cook and waitress are kind to the migrants, the truck drivers leave a big tip.

Sequence Seven—Across Arizona (2 minutes). Scene 18. After being stopped briefly by agricultural inspectors, the Joads drive across Arizona, through Indian villages and herds of sheep.

Sequence Eight—The Joads See California (2 minutes). Scene 19. The Joads reach the Arizona–California border and are awed by the desert and mountains. 20. The men of the Joad party cavort in the Colorado River.

Sequence Nine—California Sees the Joads (1 minute). Scene 21. Two contemptuous filling station attendants describe the Okies as subhuman.

Sequence Ten—Crossing the Desert: Granma's Death (6 minutes). Scene 22. Tom and Al talk about the difficulties of crossing the desert, while Ruthie and Winfield look for bones, Ma comforts Granma, and Connie complains to Rosasharn about coming on this trip instead of studying to be a radio mechanic. 23. California agricultural inspectors try to make the Joads unload the truck, but let them go when Ma protests that Granma is deathly ill. 24. The family arrives in the beautiful part of California and gazes with wonder at the Tehachapi Valley, but the experience is spoiled by Ma's revelation that Granma had died even before the California inspectors had stopped them.

Sequence Eleven—Welcome to California (2 minutes). Scene 25. In an unidentified town, a cop from Oklahoma is friendly for a minute, but quickly freezes up and orders the Joads out of town by nightfall.

Sequence Twelve—Hooverville (14 minutes). Scene 26. The Joads drive into the Hooverville and see the sorry condition of the people and huts there. 27. Ma is besieged by hungry children when she tries to cook a stew for the family. 28. A contractor attempting to hire fruit pickers is challenged by Floyd, a migrant. The contractor has a deputy attempt to arrest Floyd; but Floyd knocks the deputy down and flees. When the deputy attempts to follow and shoots a woman, Tom knocks him unconscious. Casy tells Tom to hide and takes the blame for the incident. The deputies drive off with him. 29. Tom comes out of hiding and tells the family to pack up because a mob will burn the camp; it is discovered that Rosasharn's husband Connie has taken off. 30. A mob from the town forces the Joads to turn the truck around and go the other direction.

Sequence Thirteen—The Keene Ranch (22 minutes). Scene 31. Tom and Al are fixing a tire when a man drives up and offers the family work picking peaches. 32. Migrant trucks are lined up outside the ranch gate, surrounded by a murmuring mob. 33. The Joads are checked against lists before being allowed to work and are told to mind their own business. 34. The men and children join a gaunt line of pickers headed for the grove while Ma and Rosasharn attempt to clean up a filthy cabin. 35. The Joads at dinner complain about the small amount of food their day's wages bought; Tom decides to go outside and find out what the trouble is. 36. A guard tells Tom to go back to the cabin or he will be taken back. 37. Tom slips under the wire fence and finds Casy with some others in a tent and learns that they are leading a strike against the ranch. Casy asks Tom to bring out those in the camp, but Tom doubts that they will come. Disturbed by noises outside, the group disperses. 38. Fleeing under a bridge, Casy is spotted and killed by guards. Enraged, Tom kills a guard and escapes with a broken cheek. 39. Tom returns to the cabin, where the family tends his wound and hides him. 40. The family packs up and hides Tom under mattresses in the truck. 41. The truck is allowed to leave the fenced-in ranch.

Sequence Fourteen—The Wheat Patch Government Camp (25 minutes). Scene 42. The Joad truck runs out of gas and coasts into the camp, where the caretaker explains that here the migrants govern themselves. 43. In his office, the caretaker explains more about the self-government of the camp to Tom. 44. Ruthie and Winfield Joad explore the camp washhouse and think that they have broken a flush toilet. 45. Tom is working with two other men laying pipe, when the small farmer who employs them warns that an attempt will be made to disrupt the Saturday night dance at the camp. 46. The plot is frustrated by careful work of the camp committee, and the Joad family enjoys the dance. 47. While the camp sleeps, Tom observes two men inspecting the license of the Joads' truck. He prepares to slip away, but Ma awakens and he tells her that he must go. Reluctantly she agrees.

Sequence Fifteen—Hitting the Road Again: Ma Joad's Meditation (4 minutes). Scene 48. The Joads cannot find work around the Wheat Patch camp, so they must set out for Fresno. 49. In the cab of the truck, Ma meditates on what has happened and announces the theme of the film: "We're the people that live." 50. A long, concluding shot of migrants' trucks chugging along between groves of fruit trees.

the director:

John Ford

Sean Aloysius O'Feeney (the anglicized spelling of O'Fearna) was born in Cape Elizabeth, Maine, on February 1, 1895, to Irish immigrant parents, Sean and Barbara Curran O'Feeney. He was the thirteenth and last child of the family. As John Ford, the typically dynamic and inventive Aquarian has enjoyed one of the longest and most honored careers of Hollywood directors, winning increasing recognition while making the difficult switches from silent films to talkies (that put such pioneer filmmakers as D. W. Griffith on the sidelines) and from small-screen to big-screen pictures (that slowed down the careers of important directors like Frank Capra). Although he was a successful silent film director, Ford was recognized as a major artist only late in the 1930s for a series of pictures beginning with *The Informer* (1935), and he did not become "a legend in his lifetime" until his big-screen, color spectacles about the old West in the 1950s.

The transformation of O'Feeney into Ford occurred after he failed to win an appointment to the United States Naval Academy. He may have spent a few weeks at the University of Maine (which honored him with a Doctor of Fine Arts degree in 1939). In July 1914, at the age of nineteen, he arrived in Hollywood, where his brother Francis—thirteen years his senior—had already established himself as an actor and director of serials. Many years later, John Ford told Peter Bogdanovich that his brother had acquired the name *Ford* when he had had to take over for an actor of that name who was incapacitated on the opening night of a Broadway show.*

*This account of Ford's life draws upon Peter Bogdanovich's edited version of an interview with Ford, tape recorded at Ford's California home in 1966 and upon a filmography compiled by Bogdanovich. Both appear in Peter Bogdanovich, *John Ford,* University of California Press, 1968, which should be consulted for further details. Since almost all of the material in this short book is grouped under the titles of Ford's pictures, I have avoided the use of numerous, repetitive page references.

Sean—now Jack—learned the movie business as a property man and stunt man—often for his brother's pictures—and as an actor (he was one of the mob of Ku Klux Klansmen in D. W. Griffith's *The Birth of a Nation,* 1915). He graduated to directing in 1917. Although he speaks of his first picture as *Cheyenne's Pal,* a two-reeler (about twenty minutes), filmed May 20–23 with Harry Carey, he is credited with directing and starring in *The Tornado,* another two-reeler, which was reviewed that March. After only a few more pictures, he and Carey—who wrote their own scripts—made a five-reel feature, *Straight Shooting.* The company wanted to cut it back to two, but Carl Laemmle, who headed Butterfly-Universal, happened to see it and ordered it released as made.

Most of the twenty-five or more Westerns that Ford made in 1918 and 1919 were five or six-reelers (one starring Carey was based on Bret Harte's famous story, "The Outcasts of Poker Flat"). Ford's first important assignment was his thirty-first picture, *The Prince of Avenue A,* released February 23, 1920, one in a long series of Hollywood efforts to capitalize upon the fame of sporting figures. Ford's big chance in his first non-Western was to make an actor of pugilist "Gentleman Jim" Corbett, who had lost his title of World's Heavyweight boxing champion to Bob Fitzsimmons in 1897. Though 53 in 1920, he played the romantic lead in a preposterous tale of Irish-American politics on New York's old lower East Side.

After grinding out two more films, Ford married Mary McBryde Smith on July 3, 1920; their son and daughter have sometimes worked with Ford. Meanwhile still another brother, Edward, who has often worked as Ford's assistant under the name of Edward O'Fearna (see the credits on *The Grapes of Wrath*), had arrived in Hollywood.

In 1921 Ford left Universal, after turning out three more Westerns with Carey, two with Hoot Gibson, and one with Buck Jones, and went to work exclusively with Fox Films for the remainder of the "silent era." Jack Ford became John in 1923 for his first "A" feature, *Cameo Kirby,* starring matinee idol John Gilbert. (Until World War II, Hollywood studios produced several expensive, speculative, and highly publicized "A" features each year, but relied on the smaller and steadier profits from the low-budget, quickly-filmed "B" pictures to avoid disastrous fluctuations in income. The pro-

motion of a director from "B" to "A" films was an honor that not
all proved equal to.) Ford's first big break came, however, the next
year (1925) with *The Iron Horse,* Fox's epic challenge to Famous
Players-Lasky's enormously successful *The Covered Wagon*
(1923), directed by James Cruze from Emerson Hough's best-
selling novel—the picture that launched the first era of the "Big
Western."

The Iron Horse, a lively fantasy about the building of the first
transcontinental railroad, remains Ford's longest picture (2 hours
and 40 minutes with 275 subtitles). Although the plot is a tissue
of incredible coincidences, the film remains remarkable for the outdoor photography that has become the hallmark of Ford's greatest
films (critics were already praising his painterly "framing" of his
scenes). Filmed in the Nevada desert, it helped establish the
practice of shooting "on location"; and it was one of the first works
to capitalize upon the success of a film by turning the screenplay
into a novel.

Only two more of Ford's silent films were of special interest.
Three Bad Men (1926), filmed at Jackson Hole, Wyoming, was
distinguished by a famous landrush scene that Ford told Bogdanovich is still being cut into other pictures and TV shows. *Four Sons*
(1928) is based on an I. A. R. Wylie story that Ford insisted on
filming. The lachrymose tale about the breakup of a family (like
The Grapes of Wrath) was a tremendous money-maker. It was also
the first film in which critics like Paul Rotha found evidences of
the "poetic quality" of his major pictures of the 1930s.

The switch to talkies came with a three-reeler, *Napoleon's Bar-
ber* (1928), followed by the feature-length *The Black Watch,* which
Ford has always disliked because of the long, talky sequences directed by British actor Lumsden Hare. (Hollywood producers in
the early days of the talkies were obsessed with the notion—satirized
in Kaufman and Hart's *Once in a Lifetime*—that stage personalities
had to be imported to teach the films how to talk.) Ford established
himself, however, as one of the leading directors of sound films with
his third talking feature, *Men Without Women* (1930), his first
collaboration with script writer Dudley Nichols and the first film
actually shot on a submarine. (It is also the first that Andrew Sarris
singles out as entitling Ford to recognition as a "pantheon director."
Of all Ford's silent films, only *The Iron Horse* receives prominent

attention in "Film as Art," the first volume of the incomplete *The Film Index.*)

Of the other twelve pictures that Ford made between 1930 and 1934, Sarris lists six as outstanding (*Arrowsmith*—from Sinclair Lewis's Pulitzer-Prize–winning novel and Ford's first film away from Fox since 1921—*Up the River, Air Mail, The Lost Patrol, Doctor Bull* and *Judge Priest*—the last two starring Will Rogers), but agrees with other critics that 1935 was Ford's first really big year. Then he directed the most famous of the pictures in which he worked with Rogers (*Steamboat Round the Bend*—given delayed release after Rogers's death in an airplane crash), *The Whole Town's Talking,* and *The Informer,* based on Liam O'Flaherty's novel about an Irishman who betrays a fellow countryman to the British during the Sinn Fein rebellion in 1922. Victor McLaglen starred as Gypo Nolan.

The Informer has become a Hollywood legend. Ford and script writer Dudley Nichols had wanted to make it for years. Apparently RKO finally allowed Ford to make the film as a reward for the success of *The Lost Patrol* when the director agreed to take a percentage of the profits (if any) instead of a salary. The picture didn't cost much ($218,000) and was filmed in three weeks; but it was an enormous critical success—the first Hollywood talking picture to receive serious attention as a work of art. It won Ford his first Academy Award and New York Film Critics' Circle Award, as well as Oscars for Nichols, McLaglen, and Max Steiner (composer of the score).

Ford had to wait a while to repeat his accomplishment. Despite the honors heaped on *The Informer,* the seven pictures Ford made during the next three years are among his least remembered talking features, although Ford maintains that two of his favorites among them—*Mary of Scotland* starring Katharine Hepburn and the film version of Sean O'Casey's play *The Plough and the Stars*—were ruined by cutting after they left his hands. In 1939, however, his chance came to firm up his place among the immortals.

During the 1930s Ford had had no chance to direct any of the Western epics with which he had been associated in silent film days. With the coming of talkies, emphasis shifted from outdoor action films to urban stories—both drawing-room comedies and gangster pictures—and to pompous historical and biographical spectacles.

Westerns—contemptuously called "horse operas" and "oaters"—
were filmed on a "rehearsal's the shot" basis by marginal filmmakers on Hollywood's Poverty Row, chiefly for showing on double
features in small towns and at Saturday afternoon matinees.

Ford changed this whole situation overnight when for the first
time he went on location in Monument Valley, Utah (where he has
made many of his later pictures) and returned with what may be
his most important picture—*Stagecoach,* which catapulted John
Wayne to stardom. Filmmakers and critics were skeptical of Ford's
revival of the major budget Western; they said sophisticated filmgoers would no longer accept the clichés of the Western tradition.
Ford's hunch, however, was vindicated at the box office, and major
stars began trouping out of the drawing room and into the saddle to
capitalize on the rediscovered popularity of the old West. Even
Marlene Dietrich in a comeback effort (*Destry Rides Again,* 1939)
and W. C. Fields and Mae West (*My Little Chickadee,* 1940) found
box-office gold in deliberate spoofs of the traditional horse opera.
Andrew Sarris's list of the major Hollywood productions for 1938
contains not one Western, though it is heavy with such historical
schmaltz as *Marie Antoinette.* The list for 1939, however, contains
four besides *Stagecoach* (including Cecil B. DeMille's *Union Pa-
cific,* which goes over the same ground as Ford's *The Iron Horse*).
The list for 1940 contains seven—a trend was underway, though
Ford himself made no more Westerns until after World War II,
when he revitalized the trend with *My Darling Clementine* (1947).

Meanwhile, also in 1939, he directed two historical films, *Drums
Along the Mohawk* (his first color film) and *Young Mr. Lincoln,*
both starring Henry Fonda. In 1940, as well as *The Grapes of
Wrath,* he made *The Long Voyage Home,* based on Eugene
O'Neill's "S. S. Glencairn" cycle of short plays.

Although *The Grapes of Wrath* employs the Western settings
that Ford has always handled well, it is distinctly not in the tradition of the Western, nor did Ford attempt to assimilate it to this tradition. The film is much more nearly related to his social protest
works with European settings (*The Informer* and *How Green Was
My Valley,* a 1942 production about a Welsh mining town based
on Richard Llewellyn's popular novel) than to his elaborate, ritualistic Westerns. Most of the film was not even shot on location, but
on studio lots; and the occasional shots of imposing Western land-

scapes clash ironically with the action in the foreground instead of complementing it.

Ford spent most of World War II in Navy uniform at last. In 1941, besides Erskine Caldwell's bawdy *Tobacco Road,* Ford was ironically prevailed upon to film an Army training film, *Sex Hygiene,* which became a classic of the training camp circuit because of its sickening scenes of venereal infections. After Pearl Harbor, he was appointed Chief of the Field Photographic Branch of the Navy (a unit of the Office of Strategic Services), with the rank of Lieutenant Commander. He emerged from the War a Rear Admiral. In this capacity, he and a crew including Gregg Toland (cameraman for *The Grapes of Wrath*) made films for intelligence evaluation and historical records, along with three publicly released documentaries, *The Battle of Midway* (1942), *December 7th* (1943)—both of which received Academy Awards—and *We Sail at Midnight* (1943), which Ford supervised but left others to complete.

After the war, Peter Bogdanovich reports, Ford and his group began a long film on the Nuremburg trials, but it was dropped when Ford's friend General "Wild Bill" Donovan of the O.S.S. was reassigned. His wartime experiences culminated in *They Were Expendable* (1945), a long picture (136 minutes) about his friend Johnny Buckley and the heroic P.T. boat crews that Lindsay Anderson considers "a pure example of an artist's style, if ever there was one."

Ford returned to Twentieth Century Fox after the war; but his first big postwar project, *My Darling Clementine,* marked the end of his long association with the studio, except for two brief visits to make *When Willie Comes Marching Home* (1950) and *What Price Glory?* (1952, the remake of a classic of the 1920s)—both misguided efforts to revive a dated type of war comedy.

The days of the big studios were over. Major actors and directors avoided the restrictive contracts that permitted them no control over the pictures they made and prevented them from sharing the profits of their successes. They began organizing independent producing companies that made films and then negotiated for their distribution on favorable terms through major studios.

Ford joined Merian C. Cooper, whom he had known as executive producer at RKO when he made *The Last Patrol,* in organizing Argosy Pictures, which undertook as its first venture *The*

Fugitive (1947), based on Graham Greene's novel *The Power and the Glory*. Ford still considers this grim tale of a troubled priest in a police state one of his favorite pictures, though not even Andrew Sarris lists it among his outstanding ones. Ford's comments about the picture to Peter Bogdanovich indicate Ford's isolation from the public, a kind of ivory-towerism unexpected in a man who had made a career of trying to please producers and audiences: "It came out the way I wanted it to—that's why it's one of my favorite pictures—to me, it was perfect. It wasn't popular. The critics got at it, and evidently it had no appeal to the public, but I was very proud of my work."

The question of Ford's favorites among his own pictures is hard to resolve, for Jean Mitry and Bogdanovich present different lists. On the basis of an interview in France in 1955, Mitry quotes Ford as identifying *Stagecoach, The Long Voyage Home, The Informer, The Prisoner of Shark Island,* and *The Sun Shines Bright* as his favorites. At home in California in 1966, Ford told Bogdanovich that "along with *The Fugitive* and *The Sun Shines Bright,* I think *Wagon Master* [for which he wrote the original story] came closest to being what I had wanted to achieve." He also said that *The Informer* was not one of his favorites because it lacked humor, although he also said that he did still like *Stagecoach.* Of course, Ford may have changed his mind over a decade, and we must also consider Mitry's statement that he found his lack of facility in English a handicap in communicating with Ford.

The only film common to both lists is *The Sun Shines Bright* (1953), made from some short stories by Paducah raconteur Irvin S. Cobb about a small-town Kentucky judge early in the century. Ford had earlier drawn on these tales for Will Rogers' *Judge Priest* and he had directed Cobb himself in *Steamboat Round the Bend;* but he preferred the 1953 version starring Charles Winninger (once the Cap'n Andy of the radio program *Show Boat*), which he and Cooper produced for Republic Pictures, a once aggressive independent company that has since disappeared. When the picture was released simultaneously at twenty neighborhood theatres in New York City without a downtown premiere, the *New York Times'* second-string critic Howard Thompson wrote, "It would be hard to imagine a more laborious, pedantic, and saccharine entertainment package" than this work of "ambivalent piety" in which a small town was "carelessly, caustically satirized." Contrastingly, despite the critical honors that *The Grapes of Wrath* received, it is absent from any of Ford's lists of his favorites among his films.

The later chapters of the Ford story are not relevant to a study of *The Grapes of Wrath*. As his reputation has grown, his pictures have declined in quality. Despite Andrew Sarris's enthusiasm for *Wagon Master* (1950)—inspiration for the long-time favorite television program, "Wagon Train"—Ford's reputation with the public has slumped as emphasis has shifted to a younger group of filmmakers, especially Europeans.

When Ford has been left to his own devices, his films have become increasingly private. *The Wings of Eagles* (1957)—no great popular favorite—was about a friend of his, Spig Wead, who devised the baby airplane carrier; and Ford prided himself on the fact that some of the labored comic episodes were "true." (He even wanted to call it *The Spig Wead Story,* which the producers justifiably argued would mean nothing to the public.) *Cheyenne Autumn* (1964) was an elaborately publicized film that was especially close to him, but even the admiring Andrew Sarris finds the film "a failure simply because Ford cannot get inside the Indians he is trying to ennoble." Although he has remained active into his seventies, Ford has been withdrawing more and more into the past—not only the national past in his colorful Western epics, but his own past as well—an as yet unrealized project is a film about the wartime Office of Strategic Services, with its head, his friend General "Wild Bill" Donovan, probably to be played by John Wayne.

Except for *The Grapes of Wrath,* Ford has not made a major picture about a contemporary social problem. His other films about the world around him have been wartime action documentaries. As this study will suggest, the effect of Ford's direction in *The Grapes of Wrath* was to distance and universalize Steinbeck's intensely timely story. Perhaps the most revealing remark that Ford has made about himself was his reply to Peter Bogdanovich's remark about the cynical sheriff portrayed by James Stewart in *Two Rode Together* (1961), "His morality was a little ambiguous." "Isn't all our morality a little ambiguous?" Ford countered, hardly the reply of a man who has any strong commitment to the world around him.

Ford has not lacked honor from this world. He has won four Academy Awards for directing: *The Informer* (1935), *The Grapes of Wrath* (1940), *How Green Was My Valley* (1941), *The Quiet Man* (1952), as well as four from the influential New York Critics' Circle for *The Informer, The Grapes of Wrath* (along with *The Long Voyage Home*), *How Green Was My Valley,* and *Stagecoach* (1939). He has won the Venice Biennial prize twice: in 1948 for *The Fugitive* and in 1952 for *The Quiet Man.* He has served as President of the Motion Picture Director's Association and treasurer of the Screen Director's Guild. His influence has been acknowledged by other important filmmakers, including Orson Welles, who calls *Stagecoach* his "textbook," and Pietro Germi, who has called attention to the influence of Ford's patterns on his Sicilian films. Ford has won a host of honors and honorary degrees, including the United States Legion of Honor and decorations from Belgium and Italy. He has been the focus of two cults of admirers, one centering on the British film magazine *Sight and Sound* in the 1950s and the other on the French "auteurist" critics associated with *Cahiers du Cinema* in the 1960s. Recently, quite fittingly, he has been the subject of two filmed tributes: *Directed by John Ford,* written and directed by Peter Bogdanovich for the American Film Institute and shown at the New York Film Festival in 1971, and *The American West of John Ford,* a CBS-TV special produced by Denis Sanders and Dan Ford (the director's grandson), featuring Henry Fonda, James Stewart, and John Wayne, first presented on Sunday, December 5, 1971.

the production
Ford and Zanuck

When within a month of the publication of the novel, Steinbeck's agents announced that Darryl F. Zanuck of Twentieth Century Fox had paid $75,000 for the film rights (this figure—not a record—has been inflated to $100,000 by some later historians), many people supposed that he had snapped up the rights simply to shelve the book. Zanuck later admitted that many people had advised against producing the work, arguing that it would be inflammatory and widely censored; but he immediately set Nunnally Johnson to work on a script.

Zanuck was not easily intimidated. He was a Wahoo, Nebraska boy, born the same year as John Steinbeck (1902), who had come to Hollywood to be a writer and who had, by the time he was twenty-five, worked his way up to head of production at Warner Brothers studio, just as talking pictures were about to come in. (Warners pioneered talkies, and Zanuck supervised the production of Al Jolson's *The Jazz Singer* in 1927 and the first all-talking picture, *Lights of New York* in 1928.) The young "genius" inaugurated the cycle of gangster pictures with *Little Caesar* (1930) and a new wave of musical films with *42nd Street* (1933); but in the latter year he quit Warners in a dispute over depression years' salary reductions. Three days after he quit, Joseph Schenck, President of United Artists, asked Zanuck to form a company to release pictures through United Artists, which had been organized in 1919 to distribute pictures produced by Charlie Chaplin, Douglas Fairbanks, Mary Pickford, and D. W. Griffith. Thus Twentieth Century was born. In its brief year and a half of existence—during the depth of the depression—all but one of its eighteen pictures were successful. Quarrels with Chaplin—who has since become Zanuck's personal and political enemy—over the financial terms of Zanuck's original contract, however, made the situation at United Artists uncomfortable, so that when the seriously troubled Fox Films proposed a merger, Zanuck became in 1935 at the age of 33 the head of Twentieth Century Fox, one of the giants of the industry.

Zanuck worked like hell to build up Fox's flagging fortunes, specializing in frothy musicals starring Shirley Temple, Alice Faye, and Sonja Henie, and pompous biographies starring Don Ameche and Tyrone Power. In view of his penchant for catering to the public's taste for escapist entertainment, his production of *The Grapes of Wrath* came as a shock, though subsequently he was to produce pictures like *Gentleman's Agreement* (1948) and *Pinky* (1949) that touched upon the most controversial social issues of the time. He had a gift for spotting stories that bothered people's consciences a little, but not enough to incite them to action—a skillful manipulation of guilt complexes.

The subsequent history of Zanuck's battles for the control of Twentieth Century Fox makes fascinating reading but lies outside the province of this study. Our concern is with the way in which Steinbeck's novel provided him a perfect vehicle for exploiting Americans' guilt about social inequality without suggesting that anything could really be wrong with a system that could so quickly reward the talents of a Darryl F. Zanuck, who, after all, himself came from the periphery of the Dust Bowl.

The novel was the longest work to that time by a young writer whose star rose fast in the late 1930s. After publishing several novels that attracted little attention, John Steinbeck leaped into prominence with the publication in 1935 of *Tortilla Flat,* a group of whimsical stories about some raffish "paisanos" (Mexican-Americans) who lived in the hills around Monterey, California, and spent most of their time loafing and scheming to get wine. With *Of Mice and Men* (1937), Steinbeck established himself as a playwright as well as a novelist, and this work was subsequently (1940) turned by Lewis Milestone into a film that some critics (like Richard Griffith) think the equal of *The Grapes of Wrath.*

The sensational response—even before its publication on March 14, 1939—to Steinbeck's hard-hitting protest against the condition of former sharecroppers who had migrated from the Southwestern Dust Bowl to California in search of work made the novel one of the most talked about in American history. Only a few American novels—like Sinclair Lewis's *Babbitt* and J. D. Salinger's *The Catcher in the Rye*—have enjoyed the kind of both critical and popular success that *The Grapes of Wrath* has. It moved to the top of the bestseller list on May 6, stayed there for the rest of the year and remained on the list another year.

Yet few American novels have, simultaneously, been greeted with such hostility. The novel was condemned and banned in many places and actually ordered burned in East St. Louis, Illinois. Congressman Lyle Boren of Oklahoma denounced it to his colleagues as "a lie, a black, infernal creation of a twisted, distorted mind." Such a controversial work seemed an unlikely candidate for handling by an industry that had hesitated even to identify the sides in the Spanish Civil War and that was held in check by a puritanical production code, administered by the prurient and literal-minded Hays Office. The California Chamber of Commerce condemned the project; and the Agricultural Council of California, headed by C. C. Teague, who was also an official of the Associated Farmers of California, conducted in rural newspapers a campaign against the filming of the novel, calling even for a boycott of all Twentieth Century Fox releases.

At first Zanuck encouraged the censorship controversy, thinking that it would help publicize a project that hardly suffered for want of publicity; but as the picture was readied for release, he ordered that there be no local showings in California until the film had gone into national release.

Meanwhile, he veiled the production in a secrecy that would have gratified the Atomic Energy Commission. Instead of having the screenplay mimeographed as was customary, Nunnally Johnson was ordered to make only three copies—one for himself and two for the front office (Gussow, p. 84). So that reporters could not learn the story of the film version until the picture was released, Zanuck had scripts collected every night. Little is known about the shooting of the film because most of it was done under the innocuous cover title of *Highway 66*. Not much of the film appears to have been shot on location. There are some panoramic views of scenes along Highway 66 from Oklahoma to California; but John Ford has revealed that much of the shooting was done on the studio lot. The three major sets—the Hooverville, the Keene Ranch, and the Wheat Patch government camp—surely have the fresh, temporary look of studio sets.

In his zealous efforts to assure the success of the project, Zanuck assembled a first-rate group of technicians. Most of them had been with him since United Artists' days; Ford was the only Fox legacy who played a prominent part in the venture.

He seems the only possible director for the picture. Frank Capra was more specifically associated with Hollywood's few efforts at decorous social protest (*Mr. Deeds Goes to Town* [1936], *You Can't Take It With You* [1938]), but Capra was under contract to Columbia and specialized in upbeat romantic comedies with a little twist of satire in them. Ford was the only man on the Fox lot—the only man in Hollywood for that matter—who had recently been honored for a Western picture (*Stagecoach*) and a poetically tragic tale (*The Informer*), and Steinbeck's novel was a kind of nostalgic tragedy of a West whose promise had faded. Although Ford has talked freely in interviews, he has never specifically said what he thought about being assigned *The Grapes of Wrath;* his failure, however, to list this film that brought him so much honor among his major achievements suggests that he may have regarded it as simply one of those assignments that he had to carry out because he was under contract. By 1939 Ford was, after all, an established Californian himself; and he may have had reservations about stirring up too much sympathy for the troublesome migrants.

Zanuck probably relied principally on Nunnally Johnson, the scriptwriter, to realize his own intentions in the film. Johnson had come to Hollywood in the 1920s and had scripted some of Zanuck's major productions at Twentieth Century (the George Arliss costume dramas *The House of Rothschild* and *Cardinal Richelieu,* both 1934). Moving with Zanuck, he had become a producer at Twentieth Century Fox, and later he would become a director as well.

Gregg Toland, the director of photography, was also an old Zanuck sidekick, who had begun working at United Artists on Eddie Cantor's pictures. He was also one of three cameramen whom John Ford singled out to Peter Bogdanovich for praise (the others were Joe August and Arthur Miller, who tells of his relationship with Ford in *One Reel a Week*). Toland also did the camerawork for Orson Welles' *Citizen Kane* (1941), worked with Ford on *The Long Voyage Home* (1940), and became part of his U. S. Navy crew during World War II. He died prematurely in 1948.

Zanuck entrusted the musical score to Alfred Newman, the studio's Musical Director. Newman (born in 1901) was a child prodigy, who had made his reputation conducting the orchestra for Gershwin musical plays and who with the advent of sound had come to Hollywood to work for United Artists. Zanuck had taken him along when Twentieth Century and Fox merged, and he remained with the studio until he retired in 1960. He wrote some 250 scores for films and won seven Academy Awards for scoring between 1938 (*Alexander's Ragtime Band*) and 1956 (*The King and I*). The score for *The Grapes of Wrath* couldn't have been much of a chore because it consisted almost entirely of variations on the old folk tune, "Red River Valley," which did much to add to the nostalgic effect of the picture. (Another song, "I Ain't A-Gonna Be A-Troubled This A-Way," which is sung once by Eddie Quillan, would have been a better theme for emphasizing Steinbeck's intentions.) Much of the action has no musical accompaniment, because Ford didn't like too much music in his films. He was proud, however, of one effect worked out for this film: he told Mel Gussow that "Later there was this English picture [*The Third Man*] with one instrument, a zither playing all the way through it that they talked about a lot, but it was not the first time that was done. In *Grapes* Darryl used a single, lightly played accordion—not a big orchestra—and it was very American and very right for the picture" (Gussow, p. 86).

The film must have been shot rather quickly in the late summer and early fall of 1939, while there were still long waiting lists for the novel at libraries throughout the country. The film also shows signs of having been rushed through the editing process in order to ready it for a January opening in New York while the novel was still a best seller. Robert Simpson, who had also worked with Ford on *Submarine Patrol* and *Drums Along the Mohawk,* is credited with the editing, but apparently Darryl Zanuck himself supervised much of it. Ford reputedly had gone to Honolulu on vacation.

The world premiere was at New York's Rivoli Theatre on January 24, 1940. Like the novel it was derived from, the film was an immediate public and critical success. It was expected to earn back the roughly $750,000 that it had cost by April, 1940. The Rivoli engagement alone was supposed to pay off a seventh of the cost of the film. Subsequently it became Twentieth Century Fox's most profitable production of the year. The threats of censorship never came to anything.

analysis

The Grapes of Wrath poses a challenging problem for the film analyst because it is adapted from one of the most popular and most respected of twentieth-century American novels. Many distinguished films like Stanley Kubrick's *Dr. Strangelove* (1963) and Richard Lester's *How I Won the War* (1967) have been made from relatively little-known novels, while some distinguished novels like Faulkner's *Sanctuary* and *The Sound and the Fury* have provided titles for films of little consequence. Critics rarely need to pay attention to the obscure members of such pairs.

Very occasionally, however, great films like William Wyler's adaptation of Emily Bronte's *Wuthering Heights* (1939) or Tony Richardson's version of Henry Fielding's *Tom Jones* (1963) have been made from novels that are acknowledged classics. Admirers may be led from the book to the film, from the film to the book. Enough people are familiar with both to make their interrelationship important. Though fiction and film are different and autonomous arts, when great films are made from great books the two works cannot be considered in total isolation.

The Grapes of Wrath is one of these distinguished exceptions. Both John Steinbeck's novel and John Ford's film have been acclaimed as masterworks; yet, despite their use of some similar characters, settings, and situations, they are very different works, expounding different philosophies and presenting the same basic social situation, the plight of migrant farm workers in California in the late 1930s, in quite different ways. The film may, of course, be considered entirely on its own merits; its director told George Bluestone that he never read the book. Yet because the novel is still so widely read, it cannot be overlooked in a discussion of the film. Some people would even argue that the novel should provide the basis for any discussion of the film and that the film should be judged by its faithfulness to or departure from the source. Films must finally, however, be judged as films—not as transformations of material from other media, for it should never be supposed that familiarity with even a film that faithfully follows its source can serve as a substitute for an acquaintance with the original.

Besides the still widely read novel, there is in print a screenplay of the photoplay (in John Gassner and Dudley Nichols, editors, *Twenty Best Film Plays,* 1943, pp. 333–77). The relationship of this screenplay to the film as released is not clear. It is not what one would hope to find published—a cutting continuity script, that is, a description of the visuals with a transcription from the soundtrack of the publicly distributed version of the film, for it varies in many details from available prints of the film. Perhaps it derives from the original screenplay that Nunnally Johnson submitted to Darryl F. Zanuck, who reputedly made revisions. While this screenplay is much closer to the finished film than it is to the original novel, it would be misleading to use it as a basis for study of the film. While the film does follow the basic arrangement of sequences in this screenplay, there are many differences in wording. Substantial sections of the screenplay are omitted from the film; and a few scenes— notably that of the Saturday night dance at the government camp— are longer in the film than in the screenplay. Because of the important differences between novel, screenplay, and film, a chart that may prove useful in comparing these versions of the work, while also warning against regarding either the novel or the screenplay as a reliable guide to the film, is presented as an Appendix to this study.

NOVEL AND FILM

As the Appendix indicates, the film follows the structure of the novel—though many cuts are made—through Chapter 20. Thereafter major changes are made that completely alter the tone of the final third of the movie. The government camp and peach ranch sequences are reversed, and the scenes in the boxcar camp near the cotton fields at the end of the novel are dropped altogether and replaced by a short upbeat ending, showing the Joads setting out in search of work once more.

The relationship between the novel and the film has earlier been studied by George Bluestone in *Novels into Film* (pp. 147–69), which includes an analysis of the ratios between corresponding sequences in the novel and the film based on Lester Asheim's unpublished Ph.D. dissertation, "From Book to Film" (University of Chicago, 1949). My own figures differ from Asheim's because he considers 17 percent of the book devoted to "general commentary" that does not appear in the film at all; but this general commentary in the intercalary chapters is always closely related to and sometimes in the film incorporated into the Joad story, so that I consider it most satisfactory to divide both novel and film into six parts—the scenes near the Joads' Oklahoma home (sequences one, two, and three), the scenes on Highway 66 (sequences four to eleven), the Hooverville, Weedpatch, and Hooper Ranch episodes (sequences twelve, fourteen, and thirteen, respectively), and the concluding scenes (sequence fifteen).

Using these divisions, I arrive at the following figures:

Sequence(s)	Novel	Film
Sequoyah County	157 pages 25½ %	36 minutes 28%
Highway 66	155 pages 25½ %	27 minutes 21%
Hooverville	74 pages 12%	14 minutes 11%
Government Camp	104 pages 16½ %	25 minutes 20%
Peach Ranch	62 pages 10%	22 minutes 17%
Conclusion	66 pages 10½ %	4 minutes 3%

Although these figures are slightly different from Asheim's, Bluestone is certainly right in supporting Edmund Wilson's contention that Steinbeck's work can easily be transferred to the screen. If one used the screenplay rather than the film as the basis of analysis, the proportions would be even closer to Steinbeck's, because of the expansion of the government camp scenes in the film. The only significant variation between the proportions results from the filmmakers' wish to confine the Joads' California experiences to three contrasting communities and to speed up the pace of the work by cutting down on the concluding episodes.

What no figures can show, of course, is the effect of transposing the peach ranch and government camp sequences in the film and reducing the conclusion to Ma Joad's meditation. For about 60 percent of its length, the film is essentially a condensation of the novel with the language cleaned up; but the changes made in the last 40 percent of the film are of such far-reaching consequence that they make it into a wholly different, more sentimental and simple-minded and actually somewhat antagonistic work.

After a long refutation of Wilson's condescending thesis that "Mr. Steinbeck almost always in his fiction is dealing either with the lower animals or with human beings so rudimentary that they

are almost on the animal level" that would be understandable only
to careful readers of the novel, Bluestone turns to the differences
between the two works. After arguing that although the religious
satire and socio-political implications of the novel are largely muted
in the film, "the love of land, family, and human dignity are con-
sistently translated into effective cinematic images," Bluestone admits that when we move from a consideration of these changes and
the cleaning-up of the language "to the arrangement of sequences
in the final work, we have come to our central structural problem."
But he devotes only about one fifth of his 8,500 word essay to this
problem.

In summary, his argument is that the structure of the novel

> resembles a parabola in which the high point is the successful
> thwarting of the riot at the government camp. . . . From the
> privation and dislocation of the earlier episodes, the Joads are
> continually plagued, threatened with dissolution, until, through
> the gradual knitting of strength and resistance, the family finds
> an identity which coincides with its experience at the govern-
> ment camp. . . . After their departure from the camp, the for-
> tunes of the Joads progressively deteriorate (p. 165).

On the other hand, he finds that the film, by reversing the peach
ranch and government camp episodes, achieves "an entirely new
structure," which changes "the parabolic structure to a straight line
that continually ascends." He quotes Lester Asheim as saying that
the novel, "which is an exhortation to action, becomes a film which
offers reassurance that no action is required to insure the desired
resolution of the issue." Bluestone goes on to argue, however, that
"if the film's conclusion withdraws from a leftist commitment, it is
because the novel does also. . . . The familial optimism of the one
and the biological pessimism of the other are two sides of the same
coin." Thus he seems to think the cinematic inversion "justified";
by which I gather he means satisfactory in creating the same impression upon the audience that the novel does.

The word "justified" bothers me, because filmmakers are in a
position to do what they wish with the sources they are drawing
upon. If Bluestone uses the word to mean that the film reflects the
vision of the novel, I think that he is wrong.

In *John Steinbeck* (1961, pp. 97–108), I argue in more detail
than I can reproduce here that the theme of the novel is actually
"the education of the heart." By this I mean a change from the

Joads' regarding themselves "as an isolated and self-important family unit to their regarding themselves as part of a vast human family that, in Casy's words, shares 'one big soul ever'body's a part of'" (p. 101). The completion of this education is indicated by Ma's speech near the end of the novel, "Use'ta be the fambly was fust. It ain't so now. It's anybody" and by Rosasharn's offering the breast milk intended for her dead baby to a famished old man. Although the novel ends irresolutely, the final tableau "does not halt an unfinished story: it marks the end of the story Steinbeck had to tell about the Joads. Their education is complete" (p. 107). What happens next is up to the readers. Actually Steinbeck articulated the theme of the novel in one of the intercalary chapters (14):

> This you may say of man—when theories change and crash, when schools, philosophies, when narrow dark alleys of thought, national, religious, economic, grow and disintegrate, man reaches, stumbles forward, painfully, mistakenly sometimes. Having stepped forward, he may slip back, but only half a step, never the full step back (S 204–05).

The Joads have taken such a step, so that the novel is "neither riddle nor tragedy—it is an epic comedy of the triumph of the 'holy sperit.'"

Neither Ma's speech nor Rosasharn's gesture nor Steinbeck's implicit philosophizing are retained or even suggested in the film. In their place someone connected with the production (Bluestone supposes it was Nunnally Johnson, but Mel Gussow reports that after Ford had finished the picture Darryl Zanuck wrote a speech for Ma that would provide a new ending) substituted a rewriting of one of Ma's speeches in Chapter 20. The final version of the last speech in the film is Ma's reply to Pa's observation that the family is surely taking a beating:

> I know. That's what makes us tough. Rich fellas come up an' they die, an' their kids ain't no good, an' they die out. But we keep a-comin'. We're the people that live. They can't wipe us out. They can't lick us. We'll go on forever, Pa, 'cause we're the people.

The emphasis is not on *change,* but *survival.* Actually in the film the only thing that the Joads have learned from their experiences is that they've just got to accept the beating they're taking and keep on plugging along, like the land turtle in Chapter 3 of the novel. Indeed the very point of this final speech (we will examine its differences from Steinbeck's original later in the analysis of the film) is that those who "stumble forward"—like Casy and Tom—appear doomed to destruction. Those who push themselves—like the "rich fellas"—die out. The final point of the movie is exactly the opposite of the novel's. It is an insistence that survival depends not upon changing and dynamically accommodating one's self to new challenges, but rather upon passively accepting one's lot and keeping plodding along. The philosophy is much closer to that embodied in Faulkner's *Light in August* than in Steinbeck's novel. Ironically, it is the film rather than the novel that insists that man is indeed like the turtle that must keep plodding forward without thinking about what he is doing and thus fits Edmund Wilson's description of Steinbeck's work.

The total reversal of values from novel to film can also be suggested by comparing their beginnings and endings. The novel begins with a generalized scene—a picture of the fearful impact of a dust storm upon an entire community—but it closes with a close-up tableau of the Joad family, showing that they have learned a lesson that differentiates them from the frantic turtle. The movie, on the other hand, opens with a picture of Tom Joad, a "man against the sky" in splendid isolation from society, but closes with a picture of a group of crawling trucks—remarkably similar to a parade of turtles—in which the Joad vehicle has merged almost indistinguishably into the herd moving against a beautiful landscape seeking means to sustain themselves. (John Ford humored Peter Bogdanovich's idea that the movie was supposed to end with Tom Joad's departure, but the evidence of the screenplay and Bluestone's account is that the film was always intended to end as it does.)

The novel deals with a spiritual odyssey that moves from the general to the particular and illustrates the Emersonian principle that every man must discover his own relationship to the Oversoul. The film, quite the contrary, moves from the particular to the general and illustrates what Charles A. Reich calls in *The Greening of America* the Consciousness Two principle that individuals must reconcile themselves to their places in the appointed order and not become uppity.

Many episodes and characters from the book are dropped; some, simply because of the need for condensation. A really faithful transcription of the novel would run about twenty hours, even longer than Erich von Stroheim's futile effort to reproduce Frank Norris's shorter novel *McTeague* in his film *Greed* (1923). (Curiously while people assume that material can be assimilated more rapidly through motion pictures than print, a normal reader could finish the novel in eight to twelve hours.)

Other episodes were cut, as George Bluestone indicates, to reduce the religious and political satire, to clean up the story to meet Hays Office standards, and to eliminate a multiplicity of anecdotes; but to understand the film it is more important to consider what has been retained than what has been dropped—the problem that will presently be considered in the analysis of the film itself. Final mention should be made, however, of the effects of the reduction of the roles of some of the characters in the novel. The elimination of friendly families like the Wilsons and the Cartwrights (in the final chapters) makes the Joads appear even more isolated in the film than in the novel and mutes further Steinbeck's point about the Joads' growing out of the narrow concept of "fambly" in the blood-relationship sense to a concept of membership in the entire "human family." Emphasis is further focused on Ma Joad, Tom, and Casy by reducing the roles of the other members of the family. Al's desire to break away from the family and become a garage mechanic and Uncle John's preoccupation with his "sin" are important side developments in the novel; but they are not even mentioned in the film, so that Al is reduced to a moony adolescent who drives the truck, on which Uncle John seems simply to have come along for the ride.

SCREENPLAY AND FILM

The relationship between the published screenplay and the film matters less than the relationship of the film to the novel, because it is really accidental that this transitional version has been preserved. Since the screenplay is out of print and little studied, it may be dismissed quickly, although a few comparisons between it and the final film shed light on the intentions of the film producers.

If we ignore substitutions of nearly synonymous words, changes in the word order of sentences, reassignment of speeches, and revisions of the order of speeches within a scene, which are numerous enough for a statistical nightmare but make little difference in the long run, we find that the film reproduces about eighty percent of the screenplay. Five episodes from the screenplay are dropped, and four more are substantially altered. A similar proportion is established by the dialogue: of just about one thousand speeches in the screenplay, approximately 800 are retained with little alteration, about 180 are dropped and some 20 are replaced or significantly changed.

Three of the omitted scenes are simply transitional and were probably eliminated to speed up the film (Tom and Casy's walk to the abandoned farm (G 336*b*), a conversation about buying food on the road to the peach ranch (G 362*a*), and another short conversation about Al's looking for Connie (G 368). The conversation at the state line about Tom's breaking parole and Granma's needing to make a rest stop (G 347) is also not really essential. The only serious omission is the scene of Noah swimming in the river after leaving the family (G 353*b*), which has raised more questions than are compensated for by the slight value of cutting it to speed up the film. (It should follow scene 21 in Sequence Nine.)

The important differences between the screenplay and the film are in the four major scenes that are substantially changed. (Four montages called for in the screenplay are also substantially shortened in the film, again probably in the interests of speeding up a long film.)

The first significant omission is the deletion from scene 20 (in which the Joad men swim in the river at the Arizona–California line) of a conversation with a man and his son who are returning home from California to the Texas panhandle, so that they can "starve to death with folks we know" (G 352*b*). Perhaps this conversation—along with the scene of Noah's running away—was cut out to play down the seriousness of the situation that faces the Joads in California (they have had one warning already) and to enhance the sentimental pull of Granma's death scene.

The second scene that is substantially changed also deals with the problem of defection from the family. Just before the Joads leave the Hooverville in the screenplay (G 360*a*, scene 29), Ma accuses Al of trying to run off and find other work for himself. Several other short references to Al's desire to break away and become a mechanic are also eliminated, but this is the longest and most important omission. It seems to result clearly from a desire to play down the possible disintegration of the family.

The third and most serious alteration occurs in the conversation between Tom and the other migrants who are laying pipe and their employer, Mr. Thomas (scene 45). Nunnally Johnson put his strongest political satire into this scene, which is completely emasculated in the film. Gone is an initial exchange in which Tom says that Mr. Thomas seems "a nice frien'ly fella," and Wilkie, the other young migrant, replies, "Lotta these little farmers might' nice fellas. Trouble is they're little, they ain't got much say-so." Later when Mr. Thomas warns the migrants that the deputies plan to make trouble at the next Saturday night's camp dance, his remark that "the association don't like the government camp" is cut. Immediately afterwards Tom asks, "What *is* these reds?" and Wilkie replies, chuckling:

> Well, I tell you. They was a fella up the country named King —got about 30,000 acres an' a cannery an' a winery—an' he's all a time talkin' about reds. Drivin' the country to ruin, he says. Got to get rid of 'em, he says. Well, they was a young fella jus' come out an' he was listenin' one day. He kinda scratched his head an' he says, 'Mr. King, what *is* these reds you all a time talkin' about?' Well, sir, Mr. King Says, "Young man, a red is any fella that wants thirty cents a hour when I'm payin' twenty-five." (G 371–72).

The speech is slightly condensed and cleaned up from one made by Wilkie's father in the novel, just after Thomas has walked away. The original, in which the rancher is named Hines, ends up, "Well, Jesus, Mr. Hines. I ain't a son-of-a-bitch; but if that's what a red is—why, I want thirty cents an hour. Ever'body does. Hell, Mr. Hines, we're all reds.'" "Me, too, I guess," Tom Joad adds (S 407). Even the milder version is gone from the film, along with all other mentions of "reds" except in Tom's question. When he asks it in the film, Mr. Thomas is still present and turns it aside quickly with the fretful remark, "I ain't talkin' about that one way or the other." He speaks here for the filmmakers.

Although there are more changes in the Saturday night dance episode (scene 46) than in any other, they are not of much consequence; for in novel, screenplay, and film the point is that the threat to the camp is broken up by cooperative action of the migrants without resorting to violence. John Ford seems simply to have expanded the scene in order to get a little music and fun-filled action into a work that is going to become very talky during its last few minutes. (Ford's reservation about *The Informer* was, "It lacks humor—which is my forte.")

The total effect of the changes from the screenplay to the film, however, is to soften things up a bit for the audience—to give it less to think about, a little more to cry over, a little more action to enjoy. While the screenplay is more coherent and harder-hitting than the film, only three deletions really seriously damage the final product—the cutting of the explanation of Noah's taking off, the toning down of the talk about "reds," and a speech of Ma's near the end suggesting that Rosasharn's baby has miscarried or been stillborn—"Try to be strong, honey. Someday it'll be diff'rent— someday you'll have another one. You're still jus' a little girl, remember" (G 377*a*). The removal from the closing scene of Al's remarks about trying to pass a Chevrolet changes the tone of the ending, but if they had been retained they would probably only have confused the audience and dissipated the effectiveness of Ma's moment of triumph.

THE FILM ITSELF

The important thing to the large audiences that will probably continue to see the film instead of reading the book is the way in which Johnson, Ford, and Zanuck, working with materials purchased from Steinbeck, have reared a structure of their own. How well does the film work? How do the separate parts contribute to the total effect? What impression does the film leave upon the viewer?

The technique of "thematic criticism"—popular among literary critics who stress close analysis of the language of individual writings—proves useful in answering these questions. Thematic criticism searches out the theme—the point of view about man and his world (the "message" one might say somewhat militantly)—that permeates a work and gives it its affective power. Sometimes this theme is explicitly stated, as in Milton's announcement near the beginning of *Paradise Lost* that he seeks to "justify the ways of God to men." Sometimes it is only implied and may even be so ambiguous and obscure as to generate a long-running and unresolvable controversy (the hot dispute over the proper interpretation of Henry James's *Turn of the Screw,* for example).

There seems little argument that the theme of the film *The Grapes of Wrath* is announced in Ma Joad's last speech (scene 49). Even if the makers of the film had not asserted that the theme was to be found in this line—the testimony of creators is not always trustworthy—the oracular nature of this pronouncement (coming at the conclusion, but not growing out of the action) would surely suggest that Ma is playing here the role assigned to the chorus in a Greek tragedy during its final appearance after the denouement.

There is evidence, however, of the importance that the Zanuck team attached to this ending. Mel Gussow explains in *Don't Say Yes Until I Finish Talking* (a biography of Zanuck):

> Originally, in the end, Tom Joad leaves his family to become a labor organizer and activist, to do something not only for the Joads but all oppressed workers. Zanuck wanted something tidier, and he wrote a speech for Ma Joad. . . . This ended the movie on a note, many considered, of forced sentimentality, but Zanuck was—and is—proud of the speech. . . . Ford explains the inclusion: "This picture ended on a down note, and the way Zanuck changed it, it came out on an upbeat" (p. 86).

I have earlier contested the assertion that Zanuck "wrote" the speech, since it appears in the screenplay and is only slightly altered from one in Chapter 20 of the book. But the slight alterations are enough to change the meaning. George Bluestone also reports that Nunnally Johnson chose Ma's speech for the curtain line, "because he considered it the 'real' spirit of Steinbeck's book." Whoever wrote the speech at whatever time, it's clear that it's the ending that the makers of the film wanted.

Before examining this speech and its relationship to a scene-by-scene analysis of the film, we need to consider a few matters about the production.

Direction. Much controversy among film critics centers on the so-called auteur theory, which holds that a motion picture is ultimately the work of its director, who like any other artist puts his individual imprint on his productions, and that great motion pictures, like great books or paintings, are the work of great directors, or auteurs. Andrew Sarris, principal American champion of the theory, lists John Ford with Chaplin, D. W. Griffith, and Orson Welles, among his fourteen "pantheon directors," the great American auteurs.

Other critics have objected that too many people collaborate on a film for it to be recognizably the work of one man, unless as in the unusual case of Chaplin, the director is also producer, script writer, composer of the background music, and star. Sarris's theories are surely vindicated, however, by *The Grapes of Wrath*. Whatever contributions Steinbeck, Zanuck, Johnson, and the brilliant cast made to the film, every scene bears the imprint of not so much a directing intelligence as a directing sensibility. A consistent vision of life permeates the film, and this vision could only be Ford's, because whoever wrote the words and chose the incidents and put up the money, only the director could determine the way in which the words were read, the angles from which the scenes were photographed, the placement of actors and props and lights, which are finally responsible for the impact that the action has upon the audience. This claim cannot, of course, be proved in a sentence. The whole subsequent analysis of the film will strive principally to suggest how each scene reveals the consistency, the artistic strengths, and the serious limitations of this controlling sensibility.

Acting. The acting in the picture has been so often praised that detailed comment is superfluous. The successfulness of the casting of the roles of the Joad family has few parallels in American film history. Even the crowd scenes are far more successful than in most American films; the migrants at the Hooverville and in the other camps are not just anonymous bodies. Each has apparently been chosen on the basis of looking the part that he is playing voicelessly, so that the film at these points seems like the remarkable photographs of the migrants by Dorothea Lange, Walker Evans, and other photographers of the Farm Security Administration come to life (see *The Bitter Years, 1935–1941,* New York: Museum of Modern Art, 1962). Only the children in the migrant camps are unconvincing, especially in the tear-jerking scene in which they watch Ma Joad cook dinner (scene 27). The kids from Central Casting are just too healthy-looking, sharp-eyed and self-conscious to convey the effects of homelessness and malnutrition. The casting of the adults, for even bit parts like the cook, waitress, and drivers in the truck stop (scene 17), cannot be faulted. In this respect, as in others, despite its American story and settings, *The Grapes of Wrath* seems a European production.

Photography. Ford calls Gregg Toland one of the three best cameramen he has ever worked with. The crisp, clean photography makes the film a joy to watch, one of the masterpieces of black-and-white cinematic artistry that often more nearly resembles a series of lithographs than a film. (Whether or not John Ford read the novel, I suspect that he studied Thomas Hart Benton's famous woodcuts for the Limited Editions Club printing, for individual frames often resemble them. Ford admits that his principal gift always has been for the framing of a scene.) Yet there is little really inventive or imaginative camera work in the film. Ford has generally avoided the kind of angle shots that caused a sensation in Orson Welles' *Citizen Kane* (1941), also filmed by Toland. (The differences between the camerawork in these films illustrates the influence of the director.) Ford demonstrates an almost Renaissance preoccupation with straightforward, frontal, eye-level scenes. He makes sparing use of both close-ups and long shots, suggesting that much of the film was made in the studio.

Michael Burrows finds these practices typical of all Ford's work:

> One rarely sees "close-ups" of the face only, and [Ford] *never* "zooms" into a scene. John Ford's work propounds the maxim that the camera is *not* a participant (*John Ford and Andrew V. McLaglen,* p. 9).

Ford's objective use of the camera is one reason that the few scenes in which the camera does become a participant—like the Joads's first view of Hooverville (scene 26)—strike with such particular force.

Limited use is also made of montage (far less than called for in the screenplay). There are few superimpositions or other trick shots. Ford and Toland apparently preferred to break the picture into a series of discrete episodes by the use of sharply delineated fadeouts and fadeins. From the photographic point of view, *The Grapes of Wrath* is a safe, conventional, but memorable film; everyone concerned probably felt that because of the touchiness of the subject matter the film should avoid technical novelty.

Lighting. The lighting, however, is quite another story. Ford's gift for conceiving the lighting effects that he wished and getting them from his technicians at least matches his gift for framing a scene. (One can surely believe that as a boy he wanted to be a painter; few directors have "painted with film" the way that he does.) Almost exactly half of the action takes place at night or under dimly lit conditions, so that Ford had a remarkable opportunity for exploiting the possibilities of spot lighting, especially since the migrants could afford only such inexpensive means of lighting as candles and oil lamps. Ford has an extraordinary gift for employing cinematically a technique called *chiaroscuro*—an arrangement of light and dark areas in a painting to throw certain features into striking relief by having them stand out against a darkened background. Ford's compositions in *The Grapes of Wrath* resemble the striking religious paintings of the seventeenth-century French artist Georges de la Tour. The study of the application of terms borrowed from painting to cinema is still in its controversial infancy; but if Ford's *The Grapes of Wrath* may be said to exemplify a traditional style, I would surely call it Mannerist on the basis of the lighting effects, after a school that specialized in violating the decorum of academic painting for shock effect. As William Fleming explains in *Arts and Ideas* (Revised Edition, 1966), "the Renaissance dream of clarity and order became the mannerist nightmare of haunted space" (p. 445), a style indeed suited for *The Grapes of Wrath,* which concerns uprooted people in a nightmare world.

Curiously, however, the use of mannerist techniques tends to blunt the social impact of the story. The mannerist—as Fleming also explains—holds the mirror up not to nature, but art. If *The Grapes of Wrath* had been shot in the blunt, naturalistic style of most of Alfred Hitchcock's films, it would have been unbearable. (Hitchcock teases us into accepting preposterous stories because they appear "real." This story, on the other hand, was so real that Ford had to distance it in some way from the audience.) Historical mannerism was the product of a tired, over-refined, enervated world —much like the world of the American depression; it was a style that sought some artistic solace for the overbearing horrors of reality, a style that, as George Bluestone says of the film *The Grapes of Wrath,* "vaporizes radical sociology." By his manipulation of the lights, Ford converted what could have been a nerve-wracking social protest that ends in the same kind of explosion as Michelangelo Antonioni's *Zabriskie Point* (1970) into an artful product that resolves all the transient violence in a serene meditation.

Editing. Four plusses for Direction, Acting, Photography, Lighting—now the minus. The poorest thing about *The Grapes of Wrath* —although probably nobody noticed in the initial excitement over the picture—is the editing. Although it is often said that a picture is made in the editing process and although Ford himself says that he likes to cut his own pictures, he apparently took off on vacation and left Robert Simpson to edit the film under Zanuck's supervision. The result is the unexplained disappearance of Tom's brother Noah from the film (the decision to eliminate his taking off must have come after it was too late to reshoot the early scenes in which he appears) and the lack of any explanation about what became of Rosasharn's baby. Even the sharp breaks between scenes that I discussed in connection with the photography may only be the result of hurried editing (superimpositions and other trick transitions like dissolves are demanding and expensive). Little advantage is taken of opportunities to switch from one scene to another by cutting from an object in one scene to a similar object in another (a device that Hitchcock often uses—note the transition on neckties in two early scenes of *Frenzy* (1972)—and the gray tones of contiguous scenes are not always matched as carefully as possible. The producer evidently took the chance that the film would be powerful enough that audiences would not notice sloppy cutting or loose ends in the story. At the time he was right, but later audiences— able to view the film less passionately—have regretted that the little extra care was not taken that might have made this exceptional picture nearly flawless.

Sound. Ford generally hates music in pictures (Bogdanovich, p. 99). Long stretches of *The Grapes of Wrath* have no musical accompaniment. Alfred Newman is one of Hollywood's foremost composers of background music, but this film gave him little to do. Most of the background music consists—as Ford enjoyed pointing out—of the old tune "Red River Valley" played on a single accordion by Dan Borzage. The choice of this sentimental song and the gentleness of the playing do much—as the lighting does—to play down the elements of social protest in the story and to turn it into a tear-jerking tribute to the forlorn defenders of a vanishing way of

life—in this way much like the characters in Ford's and other
Westerns. The score is remarkable, however, for its restraint and a
welcome contrast to overscored pictures like *Doctor Zhivago*. The
little music that is used is entirely suited to the producer's concept
of the picture, and it is wisely used to guide the emotional responses
of the audience, not to overwhelm or intimidate them.

Trying to keep in mind the contribution of photography, lighting, and music to the production, let's return to the theme.

Ma's final speech in the film comes in response to Pa's dejected
observation that the Joads have surely taken a beating. She replies:

> I know. That's what makes us tough. Rich fellas come up an'
> they die, an' their kids ain't no good, an' they die out. But we
> keep a-comin'. We're the people that live. They can't wipe us
> out. They can't lick us. We'll go on forever, Pa, 'cause we're
> the people (scene 49).

The speech derives from some remarks that Ma makes in Chapter
20 of the novel while trying to calm Tom down as they are driving
away from the Hooverville. Tom is outraged at the sadistic behavior of the deputy sheriffs and is afraid he may kill one—as he finally
does. Ma says:

> You got to have patience. Why, Tom—us people will go on
> livin' when all them people is gone. Why, Tom, we're the people
> that live. They ain't gonna wipe us out. Why, we're the people.
> We go on (S, 383).

At this point it is Tom who makes the observation, "We take a
beatin' all the time." Ma continues:

> I know. . . . Maybe that makes us tough. Rich fellas come up
> an' they die, an' their kids ain't no good, an' they die out. But,
> Tom, we keep a-comin'. Don' you fret none, Tom. A different
> time's a-comin' (S 383).

Actually almost all the wording of the final speech in the film
is Steinbeck's. The main difference is the omission of Ma's final,
"A different time's comin'" and the substitution for it of "We'll
go on *forever*," the omission of the initial injunction "to have pa-
tience," and the reversal of the order of the speeches. Also, in the
book, Ma is simply trying an expedient to calm Tom down and

keep the family together. There is no indication that the speech is carefully considered. In the film, on the other hand, it becomes a long-brooded summation of the knowledge gained from all Ma's experiences—a pronouncement toward which the whole film has been moving.

The implications of Ma's remarks to Tom in the novel are that the triumph of the rich is temporary and there is a change coming, though it may still be far off. The implications of Ma's remarks to Pa at the end of the film are that generations of the rich rise up and die out, but that the poor, humble people keep on going. There is no suggestion that this is not the way that things always have been and always will be.

Steinbeck is writing, as he is throughout the book, of the American Dream of unlimited opportunity, of the endless frontier, "the green light" of F. Scott Fitzgerald's Jay Gatsby. In the most important intercalary chapter (14), Steinbeck makes another assertion that is entirely missing in the film. Speaking to the great owners, he observes that they could preserve themselves if they could learn that "Paine, Marx, Jefferson, Lenin were results not causes," but that they cannot because "the quality of owning" freezes them forever into "I" and cuts them off from the "We" (S 206).

The film, however, reflects the traditional conservative European view that there will always be rich and poor, aristocrats and peasants, but that the aristocrats will rise, dissipate themselves and disappear, while the peasants will keep trudging down a long, hard road.

That Ford approached the material with a European vision is confirmed by one of the most revealing comments that he has made about the film. Answering Peter Bogdanovich's questions about what attracted him to *The Grapes of Wrath,* the director replied, "I just like it, that's all . . . being about simple people—and the story was *similar to the famine in Ireland,* when they threw the people off the land and left them wandering on the roads to starve. . . ." (Bogdanovich, p. 27—italics mine). Ford's seeing the plight of the migrants in Irish terms explains why the picture is closer in feeling to *The Informer* and *The Quiet Man* than to Ford's historical epics about the American West. I think it also explains one reason for the film's enduring appeal. Ford is not trying to rub American noses in a national mess (as Edward Dmytryk's *The*

Caine Mutiny (1954), for example, does); rather he is abstracting the Joads from any particular context and treating them as ageless figures of dispossessed wanderers. While Ford's treatment lacks much of the sting of Steinbeck's novel, it has a compensating universality that makes it still timely in providing insights into, for example, the continuing conflict between the British, Protestant, "Owner" class and the native Roman Catholic, "exploited" class in divided Ireland today.

The film does not embody Steinbeck's transcendental vision of all human beings as part of one oversoul, but rather the traditional Christian concept of earthly humility and divine justice. Small wonder that nearly all sarcastic references to traditional religion and government policemen are eliminated. (It is the "tin star" deputies, the hirelings of the rich and avaricious, that make all the trouble for the migrants, not legitimate policemen—like the one who directs the Joads to the Hooverville—who resent what they must do in order to survive themselves.)

Finally the film's injunction is to stick with the system, even though things may not always work out well. Nothing is left of Steinbeck's savage indictment, "Men who have created new fruits in the world cannot create a system whereby their fruits may be eaten. And the failure hangs over the State like a great sorrow" (S 476).

To discover how Ford's vision permeates the film requires a scene-by-scene analysis without reference to the differences from the novel (except parenthetically in a few situations in which changed emphases may annoy admirers of the novel who read their interpretations of it into the film instead of treating the film as an autonomous experience).

Sequence One—Tom Joad's Return (10 minutes)

Scene 1 is one of the few long shots in the film, exactly described in the screenplay, "An Oklahoma paved highway in daylight. At some distance, hoofing down the highway comes Tom Joad. He wears a new stiff suit of clothes, ill-fitting, and a stiff new cap, which he gradually manages to break down into something comfortable" (G 334). This conventional opening scene places the film in the "road" genre with such others as Chaplin's "tramp" pictures (especially *The Pilgrim,* 1923, also about a jailbird out west) and William Wellman's *Wild Boys of the Road,* 1933. A man is entering a scene (the viewers do not yet know that he is Tom Joad), in which we are led to expect he will make some changes, though so far we know nothing about him and no techniques are used to give the scene any distinctively individual quality.

Scene 2 is outside a roadside restaurant, where a diesel truck labeled "Oklahoma City Transport Company" is parked. The driver comes out of the restaurant to the strains of "A Tisket, A Tasket," kidding with a waitress. After he gets into the truck, Tom approaches and asks for a ride. When the driver points to the "No Riders" sticker, Tom says, "Sure I see it. But a good guy don't pay no attention to what some heel makes him stick on his truck." The driver, on the spot, tells Tom to "scrunch down on the running board till we get round the bend." The truck rolls off.

This opening conversation serves at once to polarize the difference between the rich man, "some heel," and the poor, "a good guy," that will dominate the picture. The name on the truck informs us about the setting and emphasizes the idea of the movement that will be stressed throughout the picture. The juke box song dates the action in the late 1930s. Tom's handling of the incident also establishes him as a clever, resourceful person.

Scene 3 occurs in the cab of the truck. The driver questions Tom and learns that he has been imprisoned for homicide. The conversation serves further to characterize Tom by establishing that he is short-tempered and capable of violence.

Scene 4 shows Tom encountering Casy sitting under a willow tree and discovering that Casy is the preacher who baptized him. Casy explains that he is no longer a preacher, since he has lost "the sperit," and Tom explains to Casy about his crime, imprisonment, and four-year absence from his family.

The action of the film really begins with this meeting. The three short preceding scenes have served only to establish the setting and the "rich–poor" dichotomy. This scene establishes the past and present relationship between two of the most important characters in the action and makes the spectator realize the impact that recent events are going to have upon Tom, who has been isolated from them. Casy enunciates a philosophy in this scene, "I ast myself—what *is* this here call, the Holy Sperit? Maybe that's love. . . . So maybe there ain't no sin and there ain't no virtue. There's just what people does. Some things folks do is nice, and some ain't so nice. But that's all any man's got a right to say." This speech is useful in explaining his subsequent altruistic behavior, although the ideas are never specifically elaborated upon until Tom talks to Ma at the end of the picture. Tom has no immediate reaction except to offer Casy a drink, so that the interpolation of this irrelevant moralizing creates the impression—heightened by John Carradine's gaunt face and glowing eyes—that Casy's sort of a queer duck.

Scene 5 takes place during Tom and Casy's leisurely walk to the old Joad home. Talking about Pa Joad's behavior during a baptizing, Casy imitates Pa's behavior in jumping a fence. This action reinforces the impression that Casy is an impulsive, erratic type of person.

Sequence Two—The Deserted Joad Cabin (12 minutes)

Scene 6, in the deserted and almost haunted Joad cabin, is one of the longest and certainly the most complex in the film. It is the only one to employ flashbacks. It is also the most important scene in identifying the specific situation out of which the story has grown and anchoring it in history.

When Tom and Casy arrive and find no one at home, Tom fears his folks may be dead; but Muley Graves, a former neighbor, appears and explains that they have gone to Tom's Uncle John's to prepare—like everyone else in the neighborhood, except him—to move to California. When Tom asks, "Who done it?" Muley begins his explanation by blaming the "dusters"—the only reference in the picture to the fearful dust storms of the 1930s that ruined the farmers' crops. Then the two flashbacks reveal the way in which Muley was driven off his land. In the first an agent of the company that owns the land tells Muley that he is going to be dispossessed. (The agents of the rich almost always talk to the poor from an automobile, which isolates them from the others and serves as a symbol of mechanical power. The seated agents talking to the standing people also recalls the traditional European postures of the arrogant aristocrats and the humiliated peasants.) The second flashback shows Muley's cabin actually being tractored under by another sharecropper's son who has betrayed his people for a mess of pottage. Muley then explains that though all the others have left, he can't.

Through the use of the shocking flashbacks and John Qualen's moving performance as Muley, this scene serves to impress the frightfulness of the situation in Oklahoma upon viewers and to ready them for a social protest that never comes. One gets the feeling that the scene was prepared before the film was put into final form; for the impression made by Muley and his tale unbalances the narrative and puts strong emphasis upon a character who is never seen again. Both flashbacks serve to strengthen the rich–poor dichotomy by bringing out that those who sell out to the rich are as bad as their masters. Both the fretful man who tells Muley he must get off his land and the ill-tempered tractor driver are shown as contemptuous, potentially vicious types, either no good to begin with or unhappy at the course of action forced upon them. Muley, on the contrary, defending his land, appears a paragon of virtue with whose outrage and ultimate submission viewers can identify.

Scene 7, still at the cabin, shows Muley teaching Tom and Casy the way that they must hide out from the agents of the owners, who patrol at night. The furtiveness of the characters emphasizes the extremes to which they have been driven by the unfeeling rich. "Anybody ever tol' me I'd be hidin' out on my own place . . . !" Tom Joad laments. The viciousness of the minions of wealth is also suggested by their wanton smashing of a window in the deserted cabin.

Sequence Three—Off to California (14 minutes)

Scene 8 (a sequence may consist of only a single scene, sometimes—as in some of Godard's films—of only a single shot) shows the Joad family at breakfast, listening to Uncle John read one of the handbills saying that workers are wanted in California. Ma spots Tom and Casy outside, and there is a tender reunion between them, during which she ascertains that Tom has not been hurt and hardened by his prison experiences. In succession the other members of the family demand to know if Tom has broken out. An old Hudson sedan that has been converted into a truck appears. Tom's younger brother, Al, and his sister, Rosasharn, with her husband, Connie, dismount. They also ask if Tom has broken out and are disappointed to learn that he has been paroled. Tom learns that he is about to become an uncle. This family idyll is disrupted by two men in a convertible who remind Uncle John that they are "Comin' through here tomorrow."

This scene is extremely important to the narrative and psychological development of the picture. The strong emphasis upon the lying handbills and the ruthlessness of the men who are driving the Joads off the land, both distinctive to the film, reinforce the already strong sense that the viewer has of the contempt of the rich exploiters for the ingenuous poor. The naiveté of the sharecroppers is stressed by the family's insistence that Tom must have broken out of prison—they only expect what they can get for themselves. Ma's more perceptive questions bring out a hitherto unsuspected gentleness in Tom Joad, beneath his gruff exterior. The scene establishes the Joads as nice, respectful, proud, yet self-effacing people, far more like European peasants than rowdy American backwoodsmen.

Scene 9, the next daybreak, shows the Joads loading the truck. Ma moons briefly over the few frivolous souvenirs that she has acquired during a life of privation and discards most of them. Ma's nostalgic contemplation of her souvenirs establishes that despite the nasty self-vindications of the service station attendants along the road, the Okies are indeed human beings, who have the same feelings and emotions as other people despite the hardships of their lives. The scene crystallizes the sentimental veneration of simple people that will color the entire film.

In scene 10, as the strains of "Red River Valley" rise—there has been no background music through most of this sequence—the family is boarding the truck, when Grampa revolts and refuses to go. Finally he is subdued by the children's soothing syrup. As the truck starts to leave the family invites Casy to join them. In relationship to the thematic emphasis in the film, this scene is one of the least necessary and most mood-shattering. While it does provide some comic relief at a tearful juncture, it is so long and raffish that it undermines the effect of Ma's preceding scene.

The scene illustrates one of the problems that rises in trying to film a novel. Because the form of the film is not finally determined until it is edited, expensive scenes may be shot that do not fit into the final film, but that cannot be retaken, perhaps because the cast is dispersed. In the novel Grampa's revolt stressed the point that the older the sharecropper, the more difficulty he had making a break with the past and accepting new conditions. Since, however, this theme is not emphasized in the picture, the scenes that develop it in the novel are mostly omitted. Because of its comic value, this one was retained, even though from the viewpoint of the thematic unity of the film it could be better to make a short, quick shift from Ma's reverie over her souvenirs to the family's acceptance of Casy to their reluctant departure from the known for the unknown. The "generation gap" that Grampa illustrates in the novel plays no significant role in the film.

Scene 11 is a brief conversation between Ma and Al in the cab of the truck. Ma refuses to look back, complaining that "I never had my house pushed over before. I never had my fambly stuck out on the road. I never had to lose . . . ever'thing I had in life." This brief scene epitomizes the family's reaction to their situation with a speech borrowed from an earlier part of the book (S 104—see Chart for Chapter 11). Still Ma does not sound vengeful; she is griping, not revolting against the situation. Buried in the novel, the speech made little impression, but moved to a prominent position at the end of a major phase of the Joads' history, it expresses the kind of resignation to forces beyond her control that Ma expresses throughout the picture.

Sequence Four—Grampa's Death (5 minutes)

Scene 12 is a brief montage of long shots, informing us of the progress of the Joad truck through Oklahoma as "City Limits" signs flash by—Sallisaw, Checotah, Oklahoma City—while Grampa suffers in the truck. Scene 13 shows Grampa being unloaded from the truck and dying, after making a brief protest. Scene 14 shows Tom reading a short identification that will be buried with the old man to assure people that he died a natural death and was not murdered since "lotta times the gov'ment got more interest in a dead man than a live one." Tom then prevails upon Casy to say "a few words" as the body is buried.

The particularly important thing about this sequence is Tom's speech, since Grampa's death provides an excellent opportunity for a pointed comment about a decadent rich society's lack of interest in helping the poor keep alive but its active interest in punishing the poor for trying to escape their desperate situation. It is all right for an authoritarian society to kill people, but not for people to kill themselves—all decision-making power must rest in the hands of the privileged few. Casy's "few words"—like some of

Whitman's lines in "When Lilacs Last in the Dooryard Bloom'd"—emphasize that Grampa is well out of the situation. It is "the living remain'd and suffer'd."

Sequence Five—At a Campground: Bad News (4 minutes)

In scene 15, following another brief montage of the migrant trucks crawling along the road, the Joads are shown camped somewhere—probably in the Texas panhandle—with a group of other migrants. Rosasharn's husband Connie, accompanying himself on the guitar, is singing a folksong with a skill that should have won him a place on the Grand Old Opry. The song, "I Ain't A-Gonna Be A-Treated This A-way," is quite appropriate for the situation and would be a good theme song for Steinbeck's novel. Pa has an amicable conversation with a man who has had to give up his "general notions" store in Arkansas, but the talk takes a dark turn when another man who has already been to California breaks in and tells them that their hopes are delusions because the work promised by the handbills isn't available. Tom Joad challenges the man and the proprietor of the camps asks if he's a "trouble-maker," but the man protests that he has just "tried to tell you folks what it took me a year to fin' out. Took two kids dead, took my wife dead, to show me." The group is shaken and breaks up for the night. Pa asks if the man was telling the truth, and Casy says he surely is. But when Tom asks if it is also the truth for the Joads, Casy says, "I don't know."

This scene is one of the narrative and emotional high points of the picture, the first of the night scenes to indicate the powerful role that lighting will play in the picture as the flickering lantern light illuminates in turn Connie singing, Pa Joad speaking proudly, the Arkansan speaking nostalgically, the returning migrant speaking bitterly, and Casy speaking hesitantly. For the first time it is clear that the Joads may have set out for California under an illusion. The bitter scenes that they will encounter are foreshadowed, but the scene also importantly structures the picture. What the returning man has told them is true for him, and his remarks will be borne out by the scenes that follow at the Hooverville and the peach ranch. But Casy's "I don't know" in reply to Tom's questions about the Joads' future intimates that there may be alternatives. Some of the people will be lost, but the fittest will survive. In retrospect it can be seen that the ambiguous ending of this scene foreshadows an equally ambiguous ending for the picture.

Sequence Six—At a Truck Stop: Good People (5 minutes)

Scene 17 counteracts the bitterness of scene 16 with one of the great upbeat moments of the movie—based on one of the few anecdotes retained from the book. Following another montage of the Joad truck steaming along against the stunning kind of scenery featured in *Arizona Highways,* the Joads are treated contemptuously by a filling station operator—still further evidence of the "money curtain" that separates the indifferent exploiters from the good folk. Inside a truck stop, however, the situation is different. A floozy-looking waitress is kidding with two truck drivers, when Pa Joad and his two youngest children enter and ask to buy a loaf of bread. At first the waitress is condescending and tries to impress the drivers with her sophistication, but she drops her sarcasm when the gnarled short-order cook tells her to sell Pa a fifteen-cent loaf of yesterday's bread for a dime. As Pa is paying for his purchase, he notices some candy and asks if they are a penny. Told they are two for a penny, he buys one for each child. The truck drivers protest that they are really nickel candies, and each leaves a half-dollar tip for the waitress, who looks after them reverently.

No comment seems possible on this tear-jerking episode except that the film destroys the irony of both the novel and screenplay version by cutting out the final line in which the short-order cook also collects from a slot machine that he thought "was about ready to pay off." Steinbeck's version seems simply to indicate that a little charity may prove profitable in the long run—a saccharine enough idea, but the film version's implication is that there is some special saintliness about truck drivers. The scene cheapens and trivializes the impact of both novel and film. In the novel, its effect is less strong than in the film, for it is only one of many interpolated anecdotes; but the retention of this one and the dropping of most of the others indicates the filmmakers' affinity for the most tasteless parts of the novel.

Sequence Seven—Across Arizona (2 minutes)

In scene 18 the Joads reach the Arizona border and explain that they intend to cross the state as quickly as possible. Another montage follows, showing the trucks passing an Indian village. The beautifully filmed scenes of the Indian village, with long shadows and figures in profile suggest an affinity between the migrants and the original inhabitants of the country who had also been dispossessed.

Sequence Eight—The Joads See California (2 minutes)

In scene 19 the Joads reach the Colorado River, border between Arizona and California, and are frightened by the desert that they see beyond it. In scene 20 the men of the Joad party frolic in the river. Except for establishing the difficulty of crossing the desert, the purpose of the sequence in the context of the picture is obscure, because of the omission of any indication of Noah's defection.

Sequence Nine—California Sees the Joads (1 minute)

The shortest sequence in the film establishes with the compression and obliqueness of which John Ford is capable exactly what the Joads are up against in California. Two redneck service station attendants in sloppily fitting uniforms (one may be Van Johnson, then a bit player) talk condescendingly about the Joads as less than human. The scene establishes the chasm between those people who are like the migrants but have found jobs and those that are still searching. Given sharp emphasis by the bright lighting of the white costumes and station against the ominous black background, this vignette brings out vividly the way in which "man's inhumanity to man" strengthens the hand of the rich exploiters by contemptuously dividing the lower class against itself.

Sequence Ten—Crossing the Desert: Granma's Death (6 minutes)

Scene 22 is an amalgam of short shots: Tom and Al comment on the difficulty of crossing the desert, Ma comforts Granma, Connie laments to Rosasharn that he didn't become a radio mechanic instead of coming on the trip, the youngest Joad children talk about the bones of those who died crossing the desert. These very dark scenes with the faces highlighted again emphasize the problems that the Joads are beginning to have with both external nature and internal conflicts.

In scene 23 the California Agricultural Inspectors attempt to make the Joads unload the truck, but Ma protests that Granma is very ill and must be rushed to a doctor. In scene 24 the Joads reach the beautiful part of California, stop the truck and gaze down into the Tehachapi Valley. When Ma is unenthusiastic, they discover that Granma was dead even before the inspectors stopped them. The scene emphasizes what will be repeatedly emphasized in other California scenes—the difference between the natural beauty of the landscape and the plight of the Joads. Ma's resourcefulness at the inspection station shows also, however, that the Joads have rare qualities of endurance that may indeed put them among "the fittest."

Sequence Eleven—Welcome to California (2 minutes)

Scene 25 opens with the Joads pushing the truck into a filling station in an unnamed city. When a cop asks them what they are doing, they learn he is from Oklahoma. At first he is friendly to them, but he becomes defensive when he realizes that they may want him to help them. He warns them that they must be out of town by nightfall. The scene shocks the audience with the realization of the way in which the migrants will be greeted in California; once again they find that men will turn against their own people to assure their personal security.

Sequence Twelve—Hooverville (14 minutes)

Scene 26 begins with the longest and most effective shot in the film—a tracking shot during which Toland's camera for once surrenders its objectivity and becomes the eyes of the Joads, especially Pa and Ma, as for the first time they view a Hooverville from the cab of their truck. As the truck moves slowly and carefully through the rutted mud between the ramshackle huts, the Joads observe the starved and haunted faces of the inhabitants. The men express despair and frustration, the women resentment and suspicion, the children a fear of the unknown. For the first time the utter hopelessness of the situation is brought home to the viewer as briefly the eyes of the migrants become his and he realizes that we are all involved.

The effectiveness of this opening shot is sustained throughout the harrowing scene 27, during which Ma Joad tries to figure out how to feed the family and still appease the hunger pangs of the strange children who gather and offer to help her. The tempo accelerates during scene 28, depicting the Joads' first encounter with the contractors who hire migrant labor. Shielded once again by a big car, the bloated, snarling contractor offers work picking fruit; but when a migrant named Floyd asks to see his credentials and warns the others that he's been taken in by such offers before, a deputy accompanying the contractor identifies Floyd as a man who was "hangin' around that used car lot that was busted into" and attempts to take him into custody. Floyd, however, strikes the deputy and flees. As the deputy tries to follow, Tom Joad sticks out a foot and trips him; the deputy fires his revolver, wounding in the hand a woman who has been an innocent bystander. When the deputy attempts to fire again, Casy kicks him at the base of the skull, then forces Tom to hide and takes the whole blame for the incident. He is driven away as the deputies survey with dismay the damage that the revolver has done to the woman's hand.

Tom sneaks back to the tent in scene 29 and warns the family that it must pack up and get out as "some of them pool room fellas figgerin' on burnin' out the whole camp tonight." As the family is packing, they discover that Rosasharn's husband has "lit out." Pa is "glad to get shet of him," but Tom attempts to console the girl who doesn't want to live without her husband.

In scene 30, back out on the road, Rosasharn fantasies that Connie may have gone to get some books to study to become a radio expert, and Ma encourages her delusion. The truck is halted by an angry mob from the town. Tom reaches for the jack handle, but Ma prevails upon him to be servile. The mob orders the truck to "turn right aroun' and head north."

This sequence is the beginning of the main action of the film; the earlier sequences have been a possibly overlong introduction, providing the information necessary for the audience to understand the rapid developments in this and the next two long episodes, in which the Joads are exposed to three new modes of communal life. Although political satire is muted, the film ultimately makes an implicit political comment by contrasting the conditions of life and the treatment of the migrants under three different modes of political organization—anarchy, authoritarian despotism, and democratic cooperation.

The Hooverville is an anarchic community, without laws, government, or even an enduring shape. In the novel, there is a punch-drunk character who is ironically called "the mayor," but even this token reference to orderly government is cut from the film. Anarchy is clearly an untenable alternative, because, as the cooking scene shows, the migrants are incapable of solving those problems that require some kind of governmental structure. Furthermore, the anarchical community is constantly at the mercy of the organized community outside; and the implication of the mob gathered at the end of the sequence is that the Hooverville is about to be destroyed and the refugees there dispersed.

The behavior of the contractor in scene 28 also reinforces one of the continuing themes of the film—the sadistic cruelty of the agents of the rich, dehumanized in their big automobiles or tractors and fawningly protected by irresponsible, club-wielding, gun-toting deputies. These people hope to keep the migrants continually disorganized and on the move so that they may be most easily exploited. The whole episode is one that can be lifted out of its context within the film and still serve as another powerful independent illustration of "man's inhumanity to man."

The picture might be far more powerful than it is if it had begun with the tracking shot of the Hooverville and had then incorporated such of the earlier material as is needed in the form of flashbacks, for this organization would provide a concentrated intensity now lacking in the first half of the film. Again the filmmakers do not seem to have given enough consideration to the best possible form for the film to take. Although they reshaped the material for the second half of the film to produce the final effect that they wanted, the first half of the film (the tracking shot occurs almost exactly in the middle of the film) remains too dependent upon the original structure of the novel.

Sequence Thirteen—The Keene Ranch (22 minutes)

The second major sequence is even longer and more complicated than the preceding one. In the very brief scene 31, Tom and Al Joad are fixing a flat tire when another man in a big car offers them work picking peaches forty miles north.

Although scenes 32, 33, and 34 are brief, they are among the most ominous in the film, for all emphasize the conspiracy of silence that engulfs the Joads as they enter the peach ranch. In 32, the trucks are lined up to drive into the ranch past a murmuring mob.

When Tom asks what's wrong, a policeman will tell him nothing. In 33, the Joads are interviewed by a boorish, sarcastic bookkeeper, who tells Tom that what's going on is not his affair. The family name and car license number are checked by a deputy, who informs the Joads nastily, "We don't want no trouble with you. Jes' do your own work and mind your own business and you'll be all right." In scene 34, an indifferent clerk hands out buckets to the men while Ma and Rosasharn stay to fix up a filthy cabin. Those that will pick join a sorry-looking procession of emaciated people moving towards the groves as if to a concentration camp. The whole group of scenes might have been inspired by Kafka, and their cumulative impact is to reinforce the idea that the California owners and their agents regard the migrants as less than human.

In scene 35, the others protest to Ma that their afternoon's work has not bought them enough food, and she complains about the high prices at the company store. Tom decides to nose around and find out what the trouble is, but Al is content to look for a girl, and the others decide to stay at home. This scene of a family meal is in distinct contrast to the one earlier in the film (scene 8), in which the family, though dispossessed, remains optimistic and cheerful. Now they are starving, nervous, depressed about the world into which they have been thrust.

In scene 36, a cocky guard informs Tom that he can't take a walk that night and that if he doesn't go back to the cabin by himself, he'll be taken back forcefully. The scene further reinforces the feeling of the contempt in which the migrants are held, while the use of a flashlight against a dark background calls special attention to the contrast between the bullying, but vacant face of the guard and the resentful, but puzzled face of Tom.

In scene 37, Tom watches for his opportunity and ducks under a section of the wire fence that surrounds the ranch; he clambers down a bank and comes upon a tent, where he finds Casy with a group of others who inform him that the reason for the tension at the ranch is that a group of migrants are striking. Casy pleads with Tom to ask those who are now picking to join the strike; but Tom argues that since the pickers are getting the money they want while the strike lasts, they'll think it's none of their business. Noises outside break up the meeting.

Scene 38, under the arch of a bridge across a shallow, swampy river, is the dramatic highpoint of the film. Tom and the strike leaders run from the tent and try to escape under the bridge, but they are spotted. The "tin-shield guards" single out Casy, who protests, "Listen, you fellas. You don't know what you're doin'. You're helpin' to starve kids." But one of the guards yells simply, "Shut up" and kills the expreacher with a blow from a club. Enraged, Tom clubs one of the deputies to death and escapes, but receives a serious wound on his cheek.

This could be one of the most powerful scenes in all cinema, but it is played in such darkness that it is hard to tell what is going on. John Ford, who usually makes his points visually, was probably frightened by the incendiary effect of this scene and deliberately tried to mute it, so that the impact of the event is conveyed through the dialogue rather than visual images. Casy's key speech, which heightens his similarity to Christ, is lost in the general confusion of the incident; and the audience really doesn't find out what has gone on until the next scene.

Scene 39 is an addition to the screenplay that is played without dialogue. Tom returns to the cabin and is helped and hidden by the family. In scene 40 the next morning, Ma and Tom discuss what has happened, and Ma reveals that the tale being circulated is that the strikers struck first. Tom says that he must go away; but in the first long speech in the film Ma begs him to stay and help her. Reluctantly, he agrees. Outside we learn from the announcement of a drop in the wages that the strike has been broken. Tom slowly recognizes the full import of what Casy said the night before. This important scene is choppy and filmed with so many medium close-ups that it is of little more than narrative significance. Here as elsewhere, Ford shows an impatience with long speeches, and the camera jumps nervously about as Ma rattles on about her need for help.

Scene 40 is one of the most suspenseful in the film. The family is packing to leave and the problem is to get Tom hidden in the truck without his being spotted by the ever alert guards. The family guides him out and buries him beneath mattresses just as the guards appear and ask what is going on. Al explains that the other man in the party was a hitchhiker who had gone away when the rates dropped. The viewer sighs with relief when the guards move on without inspecting the truck. The film offers few such moments of suspense.

Scene 41, in which the truck is actually allowed to leave the ranch compound, is anticlimactic.

Sequence Fourteen—
The Wheat Patch Government Camp (25 minutes)

The longest sequence of the picture bears the burden of its message. The preceding sequences at the peach ranch have provided an acerb commentary on the authoritarian despotism of the big owners and their sadistic minions. The kind of "solution" that they provide to the migrant problem must have seemed in 1940 uncomfortably similar to Hitler's "solutions" to Europe's problems. Clearly the filmmakers disapprove of the deputy's killing Casy, but approve of Tom's killing a deputy in retaliation; I have found few viewers who have not accepted this interpretation and rooted for the "criminal's" safe escape—despite the Hays Office's injunctions that crime (and sin) must always be punished. So swept away were people's emotions by the situation, however, that no voices of protest were raised against this violation of Hollywood's make-believe morality. Ford handles the material in a way that creates the greatest possible sentimental sympathy for Tom and Casy; and he evidently hoped to overbalance any rebellious sentiments inspired by the ranch sequence with the lyrical episodes at Wheat Patch government camp, the most lovingly filmed part of the work and the climactic tribute to the merits of democratic self-government.

In scene 42 the Joad truck runs out of gas and coasts into the government camp, where it is much jolted by a bump designed for reducing the speeds of those entering an area where kids play. The genial caretaker (played by the gifted Grant Mitchell with an aplomb that makes this one of the most memorable vignette performances in film history) explains to the astonished Joads that the camp is self-governing. In scene 43, inside his cabin, he continues the explanation to Tom, pointing out that the migrants make their own rules and that deputies cannot come in without a warrant. When Tom asks, "Who runs this place?," the caretaker replies, "Government." When Tom persists, "Why ain't they more like it?" the man's face suddenly darkens and he replies in one of the most heavily accentuated lines in the picture, "*You* find out. I can't."

If the picture can be called a propaganda vehicle, the label would have to be applied on the basis of these two scenes, which are the most outspokenly political in the picture. The caretaker's last reply to Tom is the one speech in the film which is even more bitter than its counterpart in the book—"The watchman looked sullen, 'You'll have to find that out for yourself' " (S 393). The inescapable implication is that the government should provide a paternalistic blanket for people like the migrants, but that it is prevented from doing so by the selfishness of the big owner-exploiters. The parallel to the Irish demand for paternalistic self-government is obvious, because the only possible interpretation of the scene is that enclaves must be set up by the government against the encroachments of the rich. Anything like the line in the novel, "This here's United States, not California" (S 456), is gone.

The novel and the film are diametrically opposed. The novel attacks the quasi-sacred American doctrine of "States' Rights" and insists that the Federal government does more for the people than the states (an insistence surely borne out by the performance of Oklahoma and California during the depression); the film, on the other hand, speaks for the kind of fragmentation that has occurred throughout the world since 1945, which has resulted in governmental entities scarcely larger than the Wheat Patch Camp being separately represented in the United Nations. The film insists that only small units are really capable of self-government—a hangover from eighteenth-century pastoral thought that has never, of course, been satisfactorily disproved. Steinbeck tended to be a "one-worlder"; Ford and his associates were village townmeeting men (like Ezra Pound and many other conservative twentieth-century artists).

Unfortunately, scene 44 degenerates into the kind of cuteness that also emanates from the novel. The opening shot, in which Tom Joad turns off a spigot that another camper has carelessly left running, is a gem of characterization; but the succeeding scene of Ruthie and Winfield Joads' exploration of the camp toilet is another example—like the earlier scene of Grampa's revolt—of the filmmakers' preserving the worst of Steinbeck for humorous sentimental effects.

Abruptly we move to scene 45, without any explanation of how Tom has obtained work, showing him working with the Wallaces while the stiffly-acted Mr. Thomas tells them of the threat to the Saturday night dance. This emasculated scene (see the discussion of the screenplay and the film) is one of the most wooden in the picture.

Scene 46 at the Saturday night dance almost deserves treatment as a separate sequence, except that the whole action at Wheat Patch is designed to drive home a single point. While there are many shifts of focus, I think that the whole episode must be regarded as a single scene, which gave Ford his major opportunity to improvise. Ford likes humorous scenes and lively action. *The Grapes of Wrath* afforded little opportunity for either to this point. Besides allowing the migrants a chance at last not just to outwit their enemies, but to triumph over them without having to run away as they have from the Hooverville and the Keene ranch, the dance scene provides an opportunity to show that these people, despite the privations they have suffered, have not lost their zest for living. Henry Fonda's croaking rendition of "Red River Valley" also provides insight into another unexpected aspect of the violent and moody Tom's character. Like a similar dance scene in D. W. Griffith's *Way Down East* (1921), the joyous country dance also gives the audience a breather before plunging into the final serious business of the film.

The mood changes decisively in scene 49. While the camp sleeps, restless Tom Joad sees a pair of sneaky figures checking the family's car license. Quickly he dresses and prepares to leave without disturbing the others; but Ma awakens and pleads once more that she can hide him. This time, however, Tom is determined to go. In the second of the long speeches in the film, he explains to Ma, to the accompaniment of train whistles suggesting a kind of perpetual migration, that he has no desire to kill anyone, but just wants to do something about a situation that he still doesn't understand. He delivers one of Steinbeck's key speeches from the novel, explaining to Ma that if it's "like Casy says, a fella ain't got a soul of his own, but on'y a piece of a big soul. . . . Then I'll be aroun' in the dark. I'll be ever'where—wherever you can look. Wherever there's a fight so hungry people can eat, I'll be there." Ma doesn't understand, either, but she sadly acquiesces in Tom's decision. At the end of the scene, as Tom steals away, the strains of "Red River Valley" come up for the first time since the end of the dance scene.

Some critics think that the film should end with Tom Joad disappearing across the horizon from which he appeared in the first scene. (Such an ending would complement his walking into the light at the beginning with his disappearing into the darkness at the end.) Such an ending would, however, turn the film into a picaresque "Adventures of Tom Joad, Outlaw"—a possible sequel to Twentieth Century Fox's earlier *Jesse James* (1939), in which Fonda played Frank James. The film would end even more equivocally than the novel, for some critics think, too, that Tom is leaving to go to his death, though the train whistles in the background suggest a mode of escape and a continuation of his "road" experiences.

Asked by Peter Bogdanovich about the possibility of ending the film with Tom's departure, John Ford said, "That was the logical end, but we wanted to see what the hell was happening to the mother and father and the girl; and the mother had a little soliloquy which was all right." The "logical end" would surely not have served what I have interpreted as Ford's purposes. He wanted the emphasis on the continuity of the good, plain people rather than on the bravado of the rebellious outcast. Actually Tom's long speech in this scene rather than summing up what the family has discovered from its experience, as it does in the novel, is simply a way of consoling Ma and calming her fears. We are not listening to a man setting forth a concrete program of action, but a son who is clever with words trying to reconcile his mother to a course of action she distrusts. From the very first scene, Tom has had the (Irish?) gift of saying the right thing at the right time.

Sequence Fifteen—
Hitting the Road Again: Ma Joad's Meditation (4 minutes)

Although the Joads have found the first happiness that they have known since leaving Oklahoma at the Wheat Patch camp, they cannot find work; so they must leave this oasis and hit the road once more. Scene 48 shows the procession of migrants, in a joshing mood, heading for Fresno. The migrants may be bloody, but they're unbowed.

Ma Joad, not Tom, is to have the last word in the film. Riding once again in the cab of the truck in scene 49, she delivers three speeches assembled from various parts of the book: the first pointing out that the migrants have survived and that she's not going to be afraid any more; the second that "woman can change better'n a man," the third the already quoted credo, "Rich fellas come up an' they die, an' their kids ain't no good, an' they die out. But we keep a'comin'. We're the people that live."

Coming after Tom's parting statement, the second of these speeches especially tends to water down even further the effectiveness of Tom's idealistic pronouncement. By putting final emphasis on the idea that "woman can change better'n a man," Ford definitely establishes Ma as the key figure in the action. There's little evidence in the picture that anything will come of Tom's fine talk; he simply disappears into the night. It's the women like Ma Joad who keep things going.

Scene 50 winds the action up with a demonstration of the virtues of stoic acceptance rather than idealistic action as the ramshackle trucks wind between the beautiful groves of fruit trees in one of the few long shots in the picture, reminiscent of the dividing of the wagon train in James Cruze's silent classic, *The Covered Wagon* (1923). Americans are still on the road, hunting the promised land; but there is a tremendous irony in the difference between the neat wagons and the untamed scenery of the epic of pioneering in the 1840s and the sorry-looking trucks and the neatly-manicured landscape of the 1940s. Man has done wonders in improving nature at the expense of degenerating himself. Steinbeck's point that "men who have created new fruits in the world cannot create a system whereby their fruits may be eaten" (S 476) leaps to the mind of those familiar with it as the picture ends, though such a subversive notion runs counter to the last words of the characters in the film.

The filmmakers seem really to have no more notion of the full impact of their creation than do Tom and Ma of Casy's ideas. The film *The Grapes of Wrath* is an impressive collection of pieces assembled without a full consciousness on the creators' part of the meaning of the whole. Despite all the cuts and editing, Steinbeck's story proved finally too powerful to be held within the restraints of Hollywood's cautious formula.

The Grapes of Wrath deals with, in short, what happens when people with an indomitable will to survive face almost certain destruction. Whether survival ultimately depended upon transcending one's situation (as Steinbeck suggests) or accommodating one's self to the situation (as the filmmakers' suggest), they were in agreement about the survival of the life-force, so that they could produce great, affirmative works in both media, even if they did not reflect the same concepts of the terms for human survival.

summary critique

After the Lights Came Up

Generally Americans make pictures, as they do everything else, only with a view to immediate profits. People feared that a movie which tackled such a touchy subject as *The Grapes of Wrath* would not make these profits. What a surprise it proved. It not only made money, but it gained great honors, and more than thirty years after it was filmed, when most of the films made at the same time can't even be sold to late-night television, it is still making money.

At the end of 1940 *The Grapes of Wrath* was selected as the best picture of the year by both the National Board of Review and the New York Film Critics. The *Film Daily* critics placed it second after Alfred Hitchcock's first American film, *Rebecca,* which also won the Academy Award as the best picture of the year. (Technically, especially in its editing, *Rebecca* is a superior picture.) Ford did, however, carry off the Academy Award as best director (Hitchcock was, after all, a newcomer to the scene, and the few faults of the film are not Ford's). Surprisingly, however, Nunnally Johnson and Henry Fonda were passed over by the Academy, which gave the screenplay and best actor awards to Donald Ogden Stewart and James Stewart for the now virtually forgotten film version of Philip Barry's drawing room comedy, *The Philadelphia Story.* (The genteel tradition still exercised a strong influence as this country careened into World War II.) Jane Darwell, however, received the Academy Award for best supporting actress. (It's hard to reward a man for playing a killer, but honoring a mother is different.) Ford also collected an award from the New York Film Critics for directing both *The Grapes of Wrath* and *The Long Voyage Home.*

The extraordinary critical and financial success of *The Grapes of Wrath* as novel and film might have been expected to set off a wave of imitations attempting to capitalize upon the phenomena (like the wave set off in the early 1970s by the success of Erich Segal's *Love Story* as novel and film), and probably just such a wave of *ersatz* would have followed had not a drastic change in the national situation cut the ground out from under it.

Even when Darryl F. Zanuck came to New York to accept the critics' award for *The Grapes of Wrath* as best picture of the year, he was on his way to Washington also to accept a commission in the United States Army Signal Corps and to produce a series of training films. Ford would soon be going into Navy uniform himself, and even John Steinbeck, though never officially commissioned, began to produce war-related works like *Bombs Away* (the story of a United States Army bomber team) and *The Moon Is Down* (a novel about a country under Nazi occupation).

Pearl Harbor changed every aspect of American life. Even the Okies themselves disappeared into California's burgeoning defense industries. It took the violence of war to solve the problem that men could not solve peacefully. The conditions that *The Grapes of Wrath* depicted were—to play on the title of its even more legendary competitor—"gone with the wind." Migrant labor became so scarce that California growers had to resort to the illegal importation of Mexican "wetbacks."

The Grapes of Wrath, as film as well as novel, marked not the beginning of a period of social protest but its end. Zanuck and Ford were right—though surely inadvertently—in treating the story nostalgically, for *The Grapes of Wrath* looks backward not forward. It serves to remind viewers even today not of what they must do, but where they have been.

The novel, as Alexander Cowle points out in *The Rise of the American Novel* (1949) provides "a brilliant and powerful synthesis" of most of the new features in American fiction that "have any value." The same claim can be made for the film, which was not, except for its background music, experimental in technique. It was to be overshadowed the next year by Orson Welles's *Citizen Kane,* which is generally hailed as marking the beginning of a new era in cinematic techniques. Even as a visual mode of exploring the problems of the poor, *The Grapes of Wrath* was to be overshadowed by the staccato style of the post-war Italian "neo-realistic" films like Rossellini's *Paisan* (1946) and De Sica's *Bicycle Thief* (1947). *The Grapes of Wrath* was an almost textbook summation of what its producer, director, photographer, script writer

and musical scorer had learned from distinguished careers as pro-
lific creators of both silent and sound films.

The immediate response to the film was adulatory. The film
reviews in the *New York Times* are probably more influential than
any others in the country. Frank Nugent, the *Times*'s first-string
critic, had written so derisively of Zanuck's productions that Twentieth Century Fox had canceled its advertising in the *Times*. When
The Grapes of Wrath was screened, however, Nugene wrote that
to the "one small uncrowded shelf devoted to cinema's masterworks, to those films which by dignity of theme and excellence of
treatment seem to be of enduring artistry" one had been added.
He concluded that *The Grapes of Wrath* "was just about as good
as any picture has a right to be" (*New York Times,* January 25,
1940, p. 17). Two months later, Zanuck hired Nugent for $750 a
week. He left Fox in 1944, but became a full-time script writer, col-
laborating with John Ford on many of his major postwar pictures.

Nugent was no more flattering, however, than the other re-
viewers. Probably most typical of the general response to the film
was the succinct comment in *Life* that the film "makes no compro-
mises, pulls no punches. Bitter, authentic, honest, it marches
straight to its tragic end . . . with a courage that merits a badge of
honor for the United States movie industry" (January 22, 1940,
p. 29). Only James Agee, the novelist, probably the only really
aesthetic critic of American films during the 1940s, had reservations
about the film. Agee did not begin to write his famous reviews for
The Nation until 1942, however, so that his attitude toward *The
Grapes of Wrath* can only be pieced together from later comments.
Agee wrote that while he admired John Ford, he could "at the same
time regret ninety-nine feet in every hundred of *The Grapes of
Wrath.*" Lumping the film with the screen version of William Sa-
royan's gushy *The Human Comedy,* Agee, in a discussion of Hollywood acting traditions, complained, "when there is any pretense
whatever of portraying 'real' people . . . such actors are painfully
out of place" (*Agee on Film,* 1964, II:29, 31). Agee apparently
did not care for the "newsreel" style that *Life* and other commen-
tators admired.

The present standing of the picture is no clearer than the standing of the parent novel. Some literary critics still insist with Wil-

liam Faulkner that Steinbeck is a superior journalist, while others, including the Nobel Prize committee, place him among the great writers of the century. The New York Museum of Modern Art Film Library, which until recently circulated the film, comments in its catalog that *The Grapes of Wrath* "remains one of the great achievements of the American film." Richard Griffith in an expanded edition of Paul Rotha's *The Film Till Now: A Survey of World Cinema* writes:

> This brilliant and courageous achievement, by which Ford is best known, while it made necessary changes in plot and prudent concessions to political prejudices, preserved the essence of Steinbeck's monumental epic of agricultural mass-migration. For the first time, millions of Americans saw their faces, and their fate, on the entertainment screen. . . . Difficult as it must always be to transform a work of art in one medium into an achievement of equal quality in another, Ford can be said to have succeeded in all essentials. In this film, more than in any of his 'arty' ones, more than in *The Long Voyage Home* or in *The Informer,* he strove for the look and sound of actual life. . . . Ford succeeded in producing a noble picture of emotional and social significance to every American. It understates the case to say also that *The Grapes of Wrath* contributed vitally to the political education of American voters (pp. 484–85).

One may well be skeptical of the last sentence. The very realism that Griffith and others praise seems to be precisely the quality that James Agee objects to; his theory seems to have been that film should be stylized and ritualistic—something like the ancient Greek drama. Griffith, too, cannot seem to get away from the relationship between the novel and the film and to appraise the film as an autonomous work of art.

The same shortcoming weakens one of the most influential tributes to the film, its analysis as a "remarkable" film in Siegfried Kracauer's *Theory of Film: The Redemption of Physical Reality* (1960). In a section on film and the novel, Kracauer observes:

> Among the reasons why Ford was in a position to follow the novel without betraying the cinema, George Bluestone lists the affinity of Steinbeck's main themes for cinematic expression; his insistence on conveying character through physical action; his concomitant reluctance to get inside the minds of people; and his indulgence in a scenario-like style free from meditations. . . .

He might have been even more specific on two counts. First Steinbeck's novel deals in human groups rather than individuals. . . . Are not crowds a cinematic subject par excellence? Through his very emphasis on collective misery, collective fears and hopes, Steinbeck meets the cinema more than halfway. Second, his novel exposes the predicament of the migratory farm workers, thus revealing and stigmatizing abuses in our society. This too falls into line with the peculiar potentialities of film. In recording and exploring physical reality, the cinema virtually challenges us to confront that reality with the notions we commonly entertain about it—notions which keep us from perceiving it. Perhaps part of the medium's significance lies in its revealing power (pp. 240–41).

Kracauer's arguments are also diametrically opposed to Agee's, and they have been vigorously challenged by such a celebrated film reviewer as Pauline Kael in *I Lost It At the Movies* (pp. 269–92).

The film, considered apart from the novel, has not always been greeted with enthusiasm. At the time of its release it enormously disturbed Martin Quigley, a coauthor of the Hays Office code that governed the content of motion pictures and editor of *Motion Picture Daily,* an influential trade paper. Quigley's diatribe was quoted in the *New York Times:*

The picture is a new and emphatic item of evidence in support of the frequently repeated assertion in these columns that the entertainment motion picture is no place for social, political and economic argument.

Quigley stressed that he had no reservations about the artistic quality of the picture, but that he was distressed by the subject matter:

If the conditions which the picture tends to present as typical are proportionately true, then the Revolution has been too long delayed. If, on the other hand, the picture depicts an extraordinary, isolated, and non-usual condition . . . then no small libel against the good name of the republic has been committed (*New York Times,* February 4, 1940, IX, 5).

The *Times* viewed with alarm Quigley's attitude; but the really remarkable thing about his commentary is the evidence it provides of the almost insuperable obstacles that American cinema faced in becoming a serious art if the rules governing it were to be drawn up by people as politically and artistically naive as Quigley.

While the film made its case too strongly for an early viewer like Quigley, at least one later critic finds it dated. Andrew Sarris, one of Ford's principal champions, writes in *The American Cinema: Directors and Directions, 1929–1966:*

> The New Dealish propaganda of *The Grapes of Wrath* has dated badly, as has John Steinbeck's literary reputation. Ford's personal style was particularly inimical to Steinbeck's biological conception of his characters. Where Steinbeck depicted oppression by dehumanizing his characters into creatures of abject necessity, Ford evoked nostalgia by humanizing Steinbeck's economic insects into heroic champions of an agricultural order of family and community (p. 45).

Sarris's remarks should be regarded cautiously, however, for Steinbeck's reputation has experienced a resurgence in the few years since Sarris wrote; and—however well informed Sarris may be about Ford—his criticisms of Steinbeck are based on a now generally discredited interpretation of his works originating from Edmund Wilson's *The Boys in the Back Room* (1941).

A curious feature of these adverse comments is that they concentrate on the content of the film and overlook the weaknesses of the editing that Mel Gussow says Darryl F. Zanuck personally supervised (*Don't Say Yes Until I Finish Talking*, p. 86). Zanuck appears to have been more intent on getting a hot property on to the market quickly than in taking time to do some reshooting that would have rendered Ford's vision of the little people who persistently "keep a'comin' " with complete consistency. Overwhelmed by the rushing movement of the film and the impact of the events, the first audiences were probably not even conscious of the lack of explanation of events like the disappearance of brother Noah; but later viewers who can approach the situation depicted more objectively and who may be more sophisticated about cinematic techniques are often distracted by small flaws from the total involvement that a sharing of Ford's sensibility demands.

Yet the film is still extremely popular with students of history and the cinema. Its distributors report that their many prints are booked for months in advance. Most viewers are still moved by the film, although they often find the sentimental ending a Hollywood cliché and wish that the filmmakers had concluded on a more critical note. What was almost too much for filmgoers of 1940 seems tame to a generation that admires *Blow-Up* and *The Devils*.

Any discussion of the film can only end on the same kind of note as the film itself. The Joads are still on the road as the film ends. As Ma observes, "Mebbe we'll find twenty days' work, mebbe no days' work." As Nunnally Johnson intended, the ending may be viewed either optimistically or pessimistically according to the predilections of the viewer. The movie, too, is still on the road; and each viewer's private judgment of it will ultimately be based on many considerations besides what he sees on the screen. The implications of *The Grapes of Wrath* extend far beyond the two hours one spends in the dark with the Joads.

a Ford filmography
bibliography
rental sources
appendix

a comparison of the novel,
screenplay, and film

a Ford filmography

I list only Ford's feature pictures (5 reels—50 minutes—or more). See Peter Bogdanovich's *John Ford* for a full list of his pictures, complete with credits.

1917   *Straight Shooting* (Butterfly-Universal)
       The Secret Man (Butterfly-Universal)
       A Marked Man (Butterfly-Universal)
       Bucking Broadway (Butterfly-Universal)

1918   *The Phantom Riders* (Universal-Special)
       Wild Women (Universal-Special)
       Thieves' Gold (Universal-Special)
       The Scarlet Drop (Universal-Special)
       Hell Bent (Universal-Special)
       A Woman's Fool (Universal-Special)
       Three Mounted Men (Universal-Special)

1919   *Roped* (Universal-Special)
       A Fight for Love (Universal-Special)
       Bare Fists (Universal-Special)
       Riders of Vengeance (Universal-Special)
       The Outcasts of Poker Flat (Universal-Special)
       The Ace of the Saddle (Universal-Special)
       The Rider of the Law (Universal-Special)
       A Gun Fightin' Gentleman (Universal-Special)
       Marked Men (Universal-Special)

1920   *The Prince of Avenue A* (Universal-Special)
       The Girl in No. 29 (Universal-Special)
       Hitchin' Posts (Universal-Special)
       Just Pals (Fox)

1921   *The Big Punch* (Fox)
       The Wallop (Universal-Special)
       Desperate Trails (Universal-Special)
       Action (Universal-Special)
       Sure Fire (Universal-Special)
       Jackie (Fox)

1922   *Little Miss Smiles* (Fox)
       The Village Blacksmith (Fox)—Ford's first 8-reel film.

1923   *The Face on the Barroom Floor* (Fox)
       Three Jumps Ahead (Fox)
       Cameo Kirby (Fox)—first signed by John Ford.
       North of Hudson Bay (Fox)
       Hoodman Blind (Fox)
1924   *The Iron Horse* (Fox)
       Hearts of Oak (Fox)
1925   *Lightnin'* (Fox)
       Kentucky Pride (Fox)
       The Fighting Heart (Fox)
       Thank You (Fox)
1926   *The Shamrock Handicap* (Fox)
       Three Bad Men (Fox)
       The Blue Eagle (Fox)
1927   *Upstream* (Fox)
1928   *Mother Machree* (Fox)
       Four Sons (Fox)
       Hangman's House (Fox)
       Riley, the Cop (Fox)
1929   *Strong Boy* (Fox)
       The remaining pictures are talking features.
       The Black Watch (Fox)
       Salute (Fox)
1930   *Men Without Women* (Fox)
       Born Reckless (Fox)
       Up the River (Fox)
1931   *Seas Beneath* (Fox)
       The Brat (Fox)
       Arrowsmith (Goldwyn-United Artists)
1932   *Air Mail* (Universal)
       Flesh (Metro-Goldwyn-Mayer)
1933   *Pilgrimage* (Fox)
       Dr. Bull (Fox)
       The Lost Patrol (RKO Radio)
1934   *The World Moves On* (Fox)
       Judge Priest (Fox)
1935   *The Whole Town's Talking* (Columbia)
       The Informer (RKO Radio)
       Steamboat Round the Bend (Fox)

1936   *The Prisoner of Shark Island* (20th Century Fox)
           Mary of Scotland (RKO Radio)
           The Plough and the Stars (RKO Radio)
1937   *Wee Willie Winkie* (20th Century Fox)
           The Hurricane (Goldwyn-United Artists)
1938   *Four Men and a Prayer* (20th Century Fox)
           Submarine Patrol (20th Century Fox)
1939   *Stagecoach* (Wanger-United Artists)
           Young Mr. Lincoln (Cosmopolitan-20th Century Fox)
           Drums Along the Mohawk (20th Century Fox)
1940   *The Grapes of Wrath* (20th Century Fox)
           The Long Voyage Home (Wanger-United Artists)
1941   *Tobacco Road* (20th Century Fox)
           How Green Was My Valley (20th Century Fox)
1945   *They Were Expendable* (Metro-Goldwyn-Mayer)
1946   *My Darling Clementine* (20th Century Fox)
1947   *The Fugitive* (Argosy-RKO Radio)
1948   *Fort Apache* (Argosy-RKO Radio)
           Three Godfathers (Argosy–Metro-Goldwyn-Mayer)
1949   *She Wore a Yellow Ribbon* (Argosy-RKO Radio)
1950   *When Willie Comes Marching Home* (20th Century Fox)
           Wagon Master (Argosy-RKO Radio)
           Rio Grande (Argosy-Republic)
1951   *This Is Korea!* (U. S. Navy-Republic)
1952   *What Price Glory* (20th Century Fox)
           The Quiet Man (Argosy-Republic)
1953   *The Sun Shines Bright* (Republic)
           Mogambo (Metro-Goldwyn-Mayer)
1955   *The Long Gray Line* (ROTA Productions-Columbia)—
           first in Cinemascope
           Mister Roberts (Orange Productions-Warner Bros.)
1956   *The Searchers* (C. V. Whitney Pictures-Warner Bros.)
1957   *The Wings of Eagles* (Metro-Goldwyn-Mayer)
           The Rising of the Moon (Four Province-Warner Bros.)
1958   *The Last Hurrah* (Columbia)
1959   *Gideon of Scotland Yard* (Columbia)
           The Horse Soldiers (Mirisch-United Artists)
1960   *Sergeant Rutledge* (Ford Productions-Warner Bros.)

1961 *Two Rode Together* (Ford-Shpetner Productions-
Columbia)
1962 *The Man Who Shot Liberty Valance* (Ford Productions-
Paramount)
How the West Was Won (Cinerama–Metro-Goldwyn-
Mayer, with George Marshall and Henry Hathaway)—
Ford's only Cinerama film.
1963 *Donovan's Reef* (Ford Productions-Paramount)
1964 *Cheyenne Autumn* (Ford-Smith Productions–
Warner Bros.)
1965 *Young Cassidy* (Sextant Films–Metro-Goldwyn-Mayer,
finished by Jack Cardiff)
1966 *Seven Women* (Ford-Smith Productions–Metro-Goldwyn-
Mayer)

bibliography

ABOUT JOHN FORD

Bogdanovich, Peter, *John Ford*. University of California Press,
1968, 144 pp.
The best source of information about Ford and his films. Bogdanovich, who has since become a director himself, tape recorded a long interview with Ford and researched his filmography
in studio files. The book is necessarily choppy. It may have been
published too early for any summary of Ford's accomplishments,
though he has not made a film since its publication. It is illustrated with a remarkable collection of stills from his films and
incorporates material from Bogdanovich's earlier writings on
Ford. The author has since produced a film tribute, *Directed by
John Ford* (1971).
Burrows, Michael, *John Ford and Andrew V. McLaglen*. Primestyle "Formative Films" Series Publications, 1970, 32pp.
Not really an essay but a disjointed series of notes by a British
film enthusiast, this slender and well-illustrated pamphlet is,
nevertheless, of great value because of many references to a

correspondence with Ford and his protégé, Andrew V. Mc-
Laglen, son of the star of many of Ford's great films of the
1930s.

California Arts Commission, *John Ford,* 1971.
A brochure to accompany showings of Peter Bogdanovich's film,
Directed by John Ford. Contains many illustrations from Ford's
films and much material from Bogdanovich's book cited above.

Jacobs, Lewis, *The Emergence of Film Art.* New York: Hopkinson
and Blake, 1969.
Contains Lindsay Anderson's "The Method of John Ford" (pp.
230–45), which originally appeared in the summer 1950 *Sequence,* a British magazine that Anderson (director of *If*) edited.
Anderson admires especially the wartime *They Were Expendable* and criticizes severely Dudley Nichols' contributions in col-
laborating with Ford.

Robinson, David, *Hollywood in the Twenties.* New York: Paper-
back Library, 1970.
A gossipy history that is, however, well documented and contains a good evaluation of Ford's achievement as a director of
silent films (pp. 165–68).

Sarris, Andrew, *Interviews with Film Directors.* Indianapolis:
Bobbs-Merrill, 1967.
Contains French critic Jean Mitry's interview with Ford, which
originally appeared in *Cahiers du Cinéma,* No. 45, March, 1955
(pp. 157–63), in which Ford explains some of his ideas about
directing ("The secret . . . is to turn out films that please the
public, but also reveal the personality of the director"). Mitry
had previously written a book in French, *John Ford* (Editions
Universitaires, 1954) that is almost unavailable in the United
States, as is the later "Special John Ford" issue of *Cahiers du
Cinéma* (No. 183, 1966).

————, *The New American Cinema: Directors and Directions,*
1929–1968. New York: Dutton, 1969.
A highly opinionated survey of American talking pictures,
grouped by their directors, which is lavish in its praise of Ford
(pp. 43–49), but not entirely consistent on the clarity of Ford's
attitude toward the materials that he uses in his pictures. The
major application of "auteurist" theory to American cinema.

ABOUT *The Grapes of Wrath*

Bluestone, George, *Novels into Films*. Baltimore: Johns Hopkins Press, 1957.
Contains a detailed analysis of the relationship between the novel and the film (pp. 147–69), derived in part from Lester Asheim's unpublished dissertation, "From Book to Film" (University of Chicago, 1949). Bluestone argues that the changes in the film do not really alter the tone or intention of the novel.

Burrows, Michael, *John Steinbeck and His Films*. Primestyle "Formative Films" Series Publications, 1970, 36 pp.
Like Burrows' book on John Ford, this is a loosely organized collection of snippets of information about Steinbeck's films, interlarded with some personal comments. An invaluable reference tool.

CBS News, *The Great American Novel: The Grapes of Wrath,* 1967.
Half of an hour-long television program, with commentary by Eric Sevareid, which attempts to show the contemporary relevance of Steinbeck's novel and Sinclair Lewis's *Babbitt*. The part on *Babbitt,* filmed in Duluth, is quite good; but the attempt to illustrate long quotations from *The Grapes of Wrath* with scenes of Appalachian migrants to Chicago is a dismal failure that shows a bourgeois inability to comprehend the difference between conditions in the 1930s and the 1960s.

French, Warren, *A Companion to "The Grapes of Wrath."* New York: Viking Press, 1963.
Reprints Bluestone's chapter, along with a summary of other responses to the film.

Gassner, John, and Nichols, Dudley (eds.), *Twenty Best Film Plays*. New York: Crown, 1943.
Contains the screenplay of *The Grapes of Wrath* (pp. 333–77), along with introductory comments by both editors on the films included.

Griffith, Richard, "The Film Since Then" in Paul Rotha's *The Film Till Now: A Survey of World Cinema*. Revised and enlarged edition. New York: Funk and Wagnalls, 1949, 755pp. Contains an enthusiastic account of the film as one of America's most important, along with an analysis of Ford's achievements in talking pictures.

Gussow, Mel, *Don't Say Yes Until I Finish Talking*. Garden City: Doubleday, 1971, 300pp.

An uncritical biography of Darryl F. Zanuck that needs to be checked against other sources, but contains a great deal of information about the filming of *The Grapes of Wrath*.

Kracauer, Siegfried, *Theory of Film: The Redemption of Physical Reality*. New York: Oxford University Press, 1960, 364pp. An enthusiastic account of the successful transformation of the novel into a "remarkable film" makes up part of this ambitious study that "rests upon the assumption that each medium has a specific nature which invites certain kinds of communications while obstructing others."

REVIEWS

Collier's, 105:23, January 23, 1940.
Commonweal, 31:348, February 9, 1940.
Life, 8:29–31, January 22, 1940 (illustrated).
Nation, 150:137–38, February 3, 1940.
New Republic, 102:212, February 12, 1940.
New Statesman and Nation (London), 20:86, July 27, 1940.
Newsweek, 15:37–38, February 12, 1940.
New York Times, January 25, 1940, p. 17 (reprinted in *The New York Times Film Reviews*, 3:1677–78).
Saturday Review of Literature, 21:16, February 10, 1940.
Sociology and Social Research, 24:497, May, 1940.
Spectator (London), 165:92, July 26, 1940.
Time, 35:70, February 12, 1940.

rental sources

16mm. prints of *The Grapes of Wrath* may be rented from Films, Inc., a major distributor of motion pictures to educational institutions, which has offices in Atlanta, Boston, Dallas, Long Island City, Salt Lake City, Skokie (Ill.), and Hayward, Hollywood, and San Diego, California. Consult James L. Limbacher (ed.), *Feature Films on 8mm. and 16mm.* Third Edition. New York and London: R. R. Bowker, 1971, for addresses and further information.

appendix

a comparison of the
novel, screenplay, and film

The chart on the following pages is arranged on the basis of the thirty original chapters of the novel. (A scene-by-scene outline of the film is presented at the beginning of this book. Scene numbers used in the chart are drawn therefrom.) More than half of these chapters are what Peter Lisca in *The Wide World of John Steinbeck* calls *intercalary,* that is, they make points or depict general situations that are specifically illustrated through the other chapters that tell the story of the Joad family. The chart also distinguishes between these intercalary chapters, in which the Joads do not appear and which are little drawn upon in the film, and the chapters devoted to the Joad Story, which provide the basis for the film. Page numbers on the chart refer to both the widely available Viking Press and Modern Library editions of the novel; paging differs in other editions. (Page references to the novel are preceded with an S; references to the screenplay with a G. Since the screenplay is printed in double columns, the *a* or *b* after a page number refers to the first or second column on that page.)

The Novel—Intercalary Chapters	*The Novel—The Joad Story*
Chapter 1. Description of a dust storm and its effects upon people (S 3–7).	
Chapter 2.	Tom Joad gets a ride with a talkative truck driver and admits to being paroled from prison after serving four years for homicide (S 8–19).
Chapter 3. Description of a box turtle—symbolic of the migrants—crossing a highway with great difficulty (S 20–22).	
Chapter 4.	Tom meets an expreacher, Casy, who has lost "the sperit." They discuss his loss of faith and the problems that reduced homesteaders to sharecroppers (S 23–41).
Chapter 5. Description of the taking over of the sharecroppers' land by the tractors of the big owners (S 42–53).	
Chapter 6.	Casy and Tom reach the deserted Joad farm and learn from neighbor Muley Graves that the family has been evicted and gone to Uncle John's to prepare to move to California (S 54–82).

Screenplay	Film
Dust storm incorporated into that part of Part One of screenplay based on Chapter 4 of the novel (G 336*b*).	Extent of dust storm curtailed, but it howls in background throughout scene 5.
About one-third of dialogue retained at beginning of Part One (G 334–35*a*), but truck driver's monologue omitted.	Scenes 2 and 3 follow screenplay with only slight changes in wording. Tom's last surly exchange with driver dropped.
Omitted	*Omitted*
About one-quarter of dialogue retained in Part One, rearranged and much bowdlerized (G 335–36). All references to sharecropping dropped.	Scenes 4 and 5 follow screenplay closely, with small changes in wording to clean it up further and eliminate idle conversation during walk toward cabin.
Interview of anonymous migrant with tractor driver (S 49–53) transformed, much reworded, into two flashbacks of confrontations between Muley Graves and agents of the big owners (G 337*b* to 339*b*).	Flashbacks incorporated into scene 6, which follows screenplay with some transpositions and addition of some dialogue about Shawnee Land Cattle Co. from Chapter 6 of the novel (S 65).
Tom and Casy's interview with Muley (G 337–40) follows novel, but omits many incidents and anecdotes, so that only about one-fifth of dialogue remains. Material from Chapter 5 used in flashbacks.	Frame section of scene 6 and all of scene 7 follows screenplay with small modifications and transpositions in wording.

The Novel—Intercalary Chapters	The Novel—The Joad Story
Chapter 7. Monologue of a dealer who sells used cars to the migrants (S 83–89).	
Chapter 8.	Tom is reunited with the family at Uncle John's and learns of the plans for the move (S 90–116).
Chapter 9. Description of migrants' selling and destroying possessions in preparation for move (S 117–21).	
Chapter 10.	Joads salt down pigs and otherwise prepare for move (S 122–48), put down a rebellion by Grampa, resolved to stay in Oklahoma (S 148–55), accept Casy into the family (S 138–40), and say goodbye to Muley (S 155–56).
Chapter 11. Description of the deserted farms going back to nature (S 157–59).	

Screenplay	*Film*
Omitted	*Omitted*

Order of events at family reunion shuffled in Part Two; only about one-tenth of dialogue retained. Scene family at dinner added (G 340–41), during which one mention of a handbill from Chapter 10 (S 123) is blown up into reading of handbill calling for pickers. A scene of agents warning Uncle John to be ready to leave also added (G 343*b*).	Scene 8 shows further cuts and rearrangements (childrens' mocking grandparents dropped), so that episode has little resemblance to novel. Ma's speech about being driven out (S 104) is moved to scene 11.
One paragraph (S 120) is basis for scene of Ma going over keepsakes (G 343–44).	Inset in scene 9 follows screenplay.
Only Grampa's rebellion is retained in Part Two. Muley is omitted, and Casy's addition to the party is moved to the end of scene (G 345*b*).	Scenes 9 and 10 follow screenplay with a few insignificant omissions.
Briefly suggested (G 346*a*), as family stares back at deserted farm.	As family stares back in scene 11, a dust storm rises, heightening the similarity between the film and the description in the novel.

The Novel—Intercalary Chapters	*The Novel—The Joad Story*
Chapter 12. Montage of movement of migrants westward on U. S. Highway 66 (S 160–66).	
Chapter 13.	The Joads travel across Oklahoma to Bethany and camp with the Wilson family (S 167–84). Grampa dies of a stroke and is buried by roadside (S 184–203).
Chapter 14. Steinbeck's central philosophical statement about man growing despite obstacles (S 204–07).	
Chapter 15. Montage of travel on Highway 66 (S 208–12). Sentimental incident of truck stop attendants making gifts to migrant family and being more than repaid by watching truck drivers (S 212–21).	
Chapter 16.	Highway becomes Joads' home (S 222–23). Car breaks down and family is about to break up until Ma threatens others with jackhandle (S 223–32). Tom repairs car by talking one-eyed junkyard attendant out of tools (S 232–49). At campground family disturbed by man who tells of coming back from California after seeing wife and two boys starve to death there (S 249–63).

Screenplay	*Film*
Retained as visual montage (G 346).	Montage simplified in scene 12. Sallisaw City Limits sign added and Joad truck featured.
About one-third of chapter used in Part Three, including speeches during Grampa's burial (G 346b). Wilsons totally omitted.	Scene 13 follows screenplay, but adds an explicit indication of Grampa's dying before Tom reads note.
Omitted	*Omitted*
Incident at truck stop moved to end of Part Three (G 349–50), with Pa Joad and two younger children taking over roles of anonymous migrants. Cook's name changed from Al to Bert.	Scene 16 follows screenplay exactly almost to end, where Bert's cynical remark about further payoff from a slot machine is cut.
Only conversation at campground retained, with a song by Connie Rivers added. Connie's complaint moved to Part Four (G 354a) and Ma's revolt with the jackhandle moved to Part Five (G 359b/360a). Conversation about Tom's crossing state line and Granma needing rest stop added (G 347).	Scene 15 follows screenplay version of conversation at campground almost exactly, but episode of Ma's revolt and her conversation with Rosasharn are cut, as is the dialogue added to screenplay about Tom's crossing state line and Granma needing a rest stop.

The Novel—Intercalary Chapters	The Novel—The Joad Story
Chapter 17. Description of development of new communal rules in migrant camps (S 264–73).	
Chapter 18.	Joads cross Arizona, and oldest son, Noah, decides to stay by river (S 274–85). Ma Joad first hears term *Okie* from an arrogant policeman (S 285–92). The Wilsons decide they can go no further (S 292–300). The Joads set off across the desert, and service station attendants call migrants "not human" (S 300–02). Granma dies during the trip (S 302–14).
Chapter 19. Steinbeck philosophizes about the struggle between California landowners and migrants (S 315–26).	
Chapter 20.	Granma is buried by the county, and the Joads are driven to a Hooverville, where hungry children watch Ma make stew (S 327–53). Tom slugs a deputy during a quarrel with a labor contractor, and Casy takes the blame and goes to jail (S 353–64). Uncle John gets drunk, and Connie Rivers runs away (S 353–73). The family moves out when Tom learns a mob will burn the camp (S 373–84).

Screenplay	Film
Omitted, though some details of life on road—like singing at campgrounds—added to material from Chapter 16.	Opening of scene 15 follows screenplay.
About one-quarter of material retained. Noah's desertion is simplified, but scene of swimming in river remains. Ma's unpleasant interview with the policeman is dropped. Conversation of service station attendants, trip across desert, and Granma's death scene retained.	About half of material in screenplay cut. Noah's desertion is eliminated, and conversation with family going home is dropped. Conversation of service station attendants is retained intact in scene 21, as are the trip across the desert and Granma's death in scenes 22, 23, and 24, with minor cuts in dialogue.
Omitted	*Omitted*
Report of burial dropped, but scene with talkative town policeman added (G 355–56). Scene of arrival at Hooverville and dinner there condensed. Incident with contractor retained with minor cuts. A scene is added of Ma's putting down Al's plan to run away (G 359*b*–60*a*), based on her revolt against family's breaking up in Chapter 16. Uncle John's drunken scene is dropped, and Connie's disappearance is not discovered until near end of Part Five (G 360*b*).	Talkative policeman retained in scene 25, but his sarcastic remark about hundreds of cousins is dropped. Scenes 26, 27, and 28 follow arrival, dinner, and fight scenes in screenplay, but Al's revolt is eliminated except for one now meaningless reference to Ma's holding jackhandle in scene 29, which also includes conversation about Connie's disappearance. Joads' being turned back by mob after leaving camp retained in scene 30.

The Novel—Intercalary Chapters	*The Novel—The Joad Story*
Chapter 21. Steinbeck speculates about the possibility of revolution (S 385–88).	
Chapter 22.	The family arrives at Weedpatch government camp and learns from the caretaker that it is self-governing (S 389–94). Tom has breakfast with the Wallace family and goes to work with them. Their employer tells them of a plan to raid the camp the next dance night (S 401–07). Ruthie and Winfield explore the camp toilet (S 407–11), while Ma gets acquainted with other campers (S 411–13).
Chapter 23. Description of the migrants' search for entertainment (S 444–51).	

Screenplay	*Film*
Omitted	*Omitted*
To this point the screenplay has followed the order of events in the novel; but government camp and peach ranch scenes are transposed, so that the Weedpatch (renamed Government Camp No. 9) episode is Part Seven rather than Part Six of the screenplay.	The film follows the order of the screenplay from this point forward, but Weedpatch Camp is renamed Wheat Patch and the Hooper Ranch is renamed the Keene Ranch.
A scene of the fanbelt's breaking and the truck's being pushed into camp is added to provide a new transition. The interview with the caretaker is retained almost intact; but Tom's breakfast with the Wallaces is dropped, so that the action cuts directly to the conversation with the farmer about the plot against the camp. This discussion is much shortened. Ruthie and Winfield's visit to the washhouse is retained (G 370*b*–371*a*), but Ma's morning interviews disappear.	Scene 42 follows exactly the screenplay's version of the Joads' arrival at the camp. Scene 43 follows the screenplay interview, except for a puzzling omission of reference to a campsite's having just been vacated. In scene 45, further extensive cuts are made in the conversation with the farmer. Tom's question about what 'Reds' are (G 371*b*) goes unanswered, and other derogatory remarks about migrants are cut. The latrine sequence is retained in scene 44, with further cuts in the dialogue.
Omitted	Tom's singing of "Red River Valley" while dancing with Ma is added to scene 46.

The Novel—Intercalary Chapters	The Novel—The Joad Story
Chapter 24.	The camp committee breaks up an attempt to start a riot that will enable deputies to raid the camp during a Saturday night dance (S 452–72).
Chapter 25. Steinbeck denounces the waste of food crops in California (S 473–77).	
Chapter 26.	The Joads have to leave Weed-patch because of lack of work (S 478–97). They get work picking peaches at the Hooper Ranch (S 497–519), but Tom meets Casy and learns that the family is helping to break a strike that Casy is leading (S 519–26). Deputies break up the meeting and club Casy to death, but Tom kills one of them (S 526–29). Since Tom has been wounded recognizably, the family leaves the camp (S 530–53).
Chapter 27. Montage of cotton picking scenes (S 554–57).	

Screenplay	*Film*
Much of the material is used, considerably rearranged, but not the final confrontation with the three troublemakers (four in film) and the anecdote about the workers' revolt in Akron, Ohio.	Another extensive rearrangement of the material makes scene 46 more like the account in the novel than the action in the screenplay. Dance sequence is considerably extended.
Omitted	*Omitted*
Only one line kept from first twenty pages of seventy-five-page chapter. Other material used in Part Six: the Joads go directly from the Hooverville to the Hooper Ranch. Most scenes of their reception are retained, but there are no scenes of actual picking in the groves. Tom's meeting with Casy and the subsequent murders are much the same as in the book; the scene of the family's departure is also kept, but condensed.	Scenes 31 to 41 generally follow the screenplay closely, though some incendiary speeches (G 361*b*, 365*a*) and an account of the family's high hopes (G 362*a*) are dropped.
Omitted	*Omitted*

The Novel—Intercalary Chapters	*The Novel—The Joad Story*
Chapter 28.	The family finds work picking cotton, but Ruthie spills the beans about Tom, who is hiding out nearby (S 558–66). Tom decides he must go away and has a long conversation with Ma about Casy's ideas (S 566–73). The family finds a few days' more work, and Al finds a girl friend (S 573–88).
Chapter 29. Description of the migrants' despair during the long wet season when there is no work (S 589–92).	
Chapter 30.	The rains come and the family fights to keep the camp from flooding; meanwhile Rosasharn's baby is stillborn (S 593–614). Ma leads the family to a barn on high ground, where Rosasharn nourishes an old man with the milk intended for her dead baby (S 614–19).

Screenplay	*Film*
All mention of cotton picking is eliminated, but Tom's speech about leaving (S 571–72) is used in the scene at Wheat Patch (G 376) and Ma's speech about the difference between men and women (S 577) turns up in the concluding scene in Part Eight (G 377*b*).	The screenplay is followed closely, and the wording of the speeches is very close to Steinbeck's. Tom's parting speech is in scene 47, and Ma's reflections are in scene 49.
Omitted	*Omitted*
Nothing is used of the original conclusion. A new conclusion about leaving the government camp in search of work is substituted, incorporating part of Ma's speech in Chapter 20 about the "people" going on (S 383). A passing reference is made to Rosasharn's losing her baby (G 377*a*).	Al's attempts to pass a Chevrolet are dropped from scene 49, as is any reference to the loss of Rosasharn's baby from scene 48; but Ma's speeches remain intact.